Understanding & Helping Suicidal Teens
Therapeutic Strategies for Parents and Teachers
From A Trauma Therapist

Támara Hill, MS, NCC, CCTP, LPC

Copyright © 2018 Tàmara Hill

All rights reserved.

No part of this work may be reproduced or utilized in any form or by any means, electronic or mechanical, including photocopying, recording, or by any information storage and retrieval system, without the proper and prior written permission or consent of the publisher and/or author. Except as permitted under the United States Copyright Act of 1976.

To receive a signed copy of this book, please forward your address, request, and book to Anchored Child & Family Counseling PO Box 113, Bridgeville PA 15017. Please allow between 4-8 weeks to receive your book back.

In the UK, Canada, and other countries, electronic orders of this book can be purchased from Kobo.com.

This book is not intended as a substitute for the medical advice of physicians or mental health professionals, particularly with respect to any symptoms that may require diagnosis or medical attention. This book is for the sole purpose of education.

The opinions and statements published are the responsibility of the author. All names used in example cases are fictitious and details have been eliminated to protect confidentiality.

Editorial Director: Tàmara Hill

Editor and cover art designer: Ryan Murray

ISBN: 1975870646

LCCN: 2017919119

Printed in the United States of America

Contents

Acknowledgements
Introduction

Chapter 1. Why this book is overdue for parents and teachers, page 27
- What the numbers are saying
- What my clients want
- What I believe most teens want
- What parents need

Chapter 2. Why some teens turn to suicide, page 37
- Identifying the problem for the first time
- Some reasons why teens turn to suicide
- Passive-death wishes and direct suicide statements
- Typical behavioral patterns of suicidal teens
- Typical thought patterns of suicidal teens
- Identifying thinking errors (activity #1)
- Suicidal ideation with or without a plan
- What we all should know about teens considering suicide

Chapter 3. Developing a clear understanding of teen suicide-contagion, page 83
- Red flag meetings, and collective disturbance
- A brief historical and modern view of suicide-contagion
- Social media and the influence of suicide-contagion
- Religious cults and the influence of suicide-contagion

Chapter 4. What to do and where to start, page 99
- Identifying the problem for the first time
- How parents can approach the topic of suicide with a teen
- Involving the school
- Helping teens regain stability
- Reacting with empathy
- Case study of Stephanie (activity #2)

- What teachers can do to help

Chapter 5. Pursuing mental health treatment, page 142
- Who to see for mental health treatment
- What not to say to teens you are trying to get into treatment (activity #3)
- Questions to ask on first appointments
- Residential treatment for suicidal thoughts and behaviors
- Hospitalization for suicidal thoughts
- Partial hospital treatment services
- Outpatient therapy services
- Other therapeutic services
- Involuntary(302) commitment: When a provider hospitalizes a client
- What to expect when your teen is hospitalized
- Voluntary (201) services
- Referrals and follow-up
- Community supports

Chapter 6. Safety planning from a trauma-informed perspective, page 200
- Sanctuary Model of Trauma-Informed care
- My use of the SELF-Model with a suicidal teen with a traumatic past
- SELF-Model (activity #4)
- Trauma-Focused Cognitive Behavior Therapy
- Activities from TF-CBT I have used in therapy with suicidal teens
- Development of the safety plan (activity #5)
- Crisis planning
- Debriefing: Example of debriefing

Chapter 7. Maintaining treatment services and staying organized, page 237
- The therapeutic bond
- Maintaining open communication with your teen and the therapist
- Obtaining consent and making contact with the therapist
- Maintaining open communication with virtual sessions or face-time

- Barriers to maintaining treatment with a personality or mood disorder
- Barriers to maintaining treatment with oppositional and moody teens
- Maintaining open communication with your teen's school
- Staying organized

Chapter 8. Conclusion, page 270
- The role of teachers in preventing suicide and raising awareness
- Facts for teachers about teens who are at risk for suicide
- When attempts at communication fail with resistant teens
- Why I believe integrating faith-based viewpoints is a good start

Resources
References
About the author

**Understanding & Helping Suicidal Teens
Therapeutic Strategies for Parents and Teachers
From A Trauma Therapist**

Acknowledgements

This book would not be what it is without the encouragement, support, and love of my mom. You are my motivating "internal voice." The one who reminds me of who I am, of what my mission is, and of where I should be going. Aside from God, you are everything. Thank you for always being my support and faithful partner in Christ.

To my brother for his artistic and archeological touches, thank you! You have amazing talent. I also want to thank my grandmother for her prayers and for sharing my passion with her friends and church. This book would also not be what it is without the encouragement of my clients, close confidants, and people outside of the U.S. (including "mentors") that I have had the opportunity to cross paths with. Receiving emails from people in the U.K., Canada, Austrailia, and across the U.S. who have requested a book like this was the inspiration for this work. I hope you all will see this production as a show of my unending passion to study, understand, and support families in their search for knowledge.

Grateful I can reach out to many of you.

"...But in the end one needs more courage to live than to kill himself. "

- Albert Camus

Introduction

"Raise your words, not your voice. It is rain that grows flowers, not thunder."

- Rumi

How would you feel having a discussion about suicide? What if that discussion was with an adolescent who is considering it as an option for themselves? For many parents in today's society suicidal thoughts aren't something they are too worried about. Why? Because adolescents seem to be constantly cocooned in their social media worlds fighting other battles such as cyberbullying, exposure to porn, and/or sexting. But what parents fail to realize is that with the introduction of newer forms of technology (i.e., social media platforms like Snapchat, Gab, and Viber) it can sometimes be very difficult if not impossible to figure out what is going on in a teen's world. As a result, most parents (and even teachers) are caught by surprise when a teen's suicidal thoughts and behaviors are revealed or become known through the grapevine. Once a parent recognizes their teen is considering suicide a typical emotional response is to rush into a conversation about how inappropriate, unnecessary, and dangerous the thoughts are. There is often little to no consideration of how the teen might respond and how the teen might feel about the entire encounter. I'm sure you can relate. As a loving and concerned parent who seeks only to remedy the situation and gather details so the thoughts can "stop," you might take the same approach. But I think the first step toward helping your teen is to employ a smarter approach.

There is no real way to "stop" the thoughts. In fact, most people (especially teens) will think of suicide at some point in their lives. Therefore, the goal is not to stop the thoughts. The goal is to help your teen see that they are not abnormal, that they have access to many supportive resources, and that there would be no benefit in killing themselves. Thankfully, you can learn and develop the right skills to address the topic of suicide in a calm fashion with your teen. Your ultimate goal is to offer support and help while you consider and explore treatment options. Your goal, I'm sure, is not to become your teen's enemy but rather to become your teen's partner in a battle of the mind.After about 10 years working with families I have come to believe that parents can empower themselves by learning better ways to monitor their teen's inner and outer worlds. A teen's inner world may consist of very dark, pessimistic, depressing, and suicidal thoughts. Their "outer world" may consist of more negative things such as being bullied, low self-esteem, low self-efficacy, or fears of failure. You need tools to understand their worldview. Although a teen's world can be rather depressing, they deserve to have someone (especially a trusted parent) join them in that world, even if temporarily. When you "join" forces with your teen, you help build the kind of trusting relationship they will need for the rest of their life. We must not assume that a teen's suicidal thoughts are acute or fleeting. In most cases, they are not. A teen doesn't just become suicidal overnight. Many become suicidal after years, months, or weeks of feeling depressed, hopeless, helpless, or unable to meet other's expectations. Sometimes the only hope for them is the parent-child relationship.

It is important that you also begin to monitor the interactions your teen may be having with negative peers. Negative peers can influence them to consider suicide or may be the very cause of their suicidal thoughts. The first step in monitoring interactions would be by monitoring their cell phone use, Facebook or Instagram interactions, and other social media use. Social media is the new "social hub" for today's teens. I strongly believe teens should have some degree of privacy but I also strongly believe that suicidal teens need structure and monitoring until they are able to resist suicidal impulses. If you suspect social media use has something to do with suicidal thoughts or behaviors, you certainly need to begin monitoring your teen's use. Social media apps such as TeenSafe can help you monitor social media use as well as deleted text messages, Snapchat, Facebook posts, etc. The app runs in the background of your teen's phone which means they won't know it is installed. I do encourage you to discuss this with your teen prior to installing it on their phone. They need to understand that you are not trying to undermine their privacy or right to grow up but rather, protect and support them. Most teen's respond negatively to the use of social media monitoring apps like this. But I typically encourage parents to stand their ground until they see mature and safer behaviors in their teen. You certainly would want to have a candid conversation with your teen about this if you decide to use it. You can learn more from the website: www.teensafe.org.

Despite these useful tools, teens need adults they see every single day (who truly understand their deepest needs and who will not resort to automatic punishments) to learn about the things that push them to have suicidal thoughts or behaviors. I have counseled teen clients who come to therapy very angry with the parent who decided to take an authoritarian approach (i.e., harsh, unfair, or intimidating) to their admission of suicidal thoughts. One teen confided in me by stating "I don't talk to my dad about my suicidal thoughts because he will just tell me to suck it up, get over it, and go to school and make friends. He doesn't get it. He thinks I'm trying to get attention. Well, I am but not in that way. I need help. I'm suffering here." As a licensed child and adolescent therapist and certified trauma professional, I have seen my fair share of suicidal youths like this who also internalize their thoughts and emotions to avoid adults who pressure them, judge them, or overreact. Although we can probably agree that most adolescents can be the epitome of drama, they do not always respond well to dramatic people, or worse, dramatic parents.

As a result, this book will offer ways parents can appropriately relate to and address a teen about suicide. This book will offer tips on steps you, as the parent, can take to ensure you are supporting your teen. The theories, discussions, stories, and most of the worksheets in this book are all representative of my own work with suicidal teens. You will find therapeutic worksheets and activities I find most helpful to the families I see. I will also discuss topics parents tend to approach me about following conferences, seminars, trainings, classes, and therapy sessions such as:

- identifying suicidal thoughts and behaviors,
- addressing the teen about their suicidal thoughts and behaviors,
- conversing with the teen in a way to foster open communication,
- identifying support tools,
- informing the teen's school of suicidal thoughts,
- pursuing various levels of treatment, and
- maintaining healthy and open communication with teachers and treatment providers.

It is important I add that this book is written with teachers in mind as well. Teachers can utilize some of the tools in this book with families and also learn about

the challenges families face when embarking upon the frightening reality that a teen is contemplating suicide. Once an adolescent has been identified as suicidal, it is important that you learn how to ask for help from mental health professionals and and your teen's school (if you choose to involve them).Reaching out may consist of:
- sending a letter, email, or leaving a voicemail
- contacting the Principal or a trusted teacher
- maintaining open communication every couple of weeks
- informing the school of progress or lack thereof

Another step in supporting your teen is examining the home for lethal "weapons" that can be used to assist them with suicide. Examples of "weapons" include medications that are not locked up, kitchen knives, hunting weapons, power tools or other tools commonly found in toolboxes, beauty tools such as tweezers or scissors, and other similar items in the home. You will also want to be mindful of your house cleaning products as younger teens may attempt to sniff the products to achieve a "high" or pass out. You certainly want to brainstorm the various ways your teen may attempt to harm themselves and try to remove the potential for them to use whatever is in their immediate environment.

Lock things up or donate them, give potentially dangerous items temporarily to a neighbor or family member, and avoid purchasing items that could be used to assist in a suicide until your teen is emotionally stable. For example postpone hunting or going to a gun range until your teen is emotionally stable. We certainly do not want to prevent teens from enjoying themselves or experiencing some freedom. But we do want to ensure they will not be a threat to themselves in any way. Don't give them that opportunity. Do whatever you need to do to ensure your home is safe until your teen is able to cope better.

At this point you may be wondering if you should discuss the removal of these items from your home with your teen. My common response is yes. Teens need to understand that you are no longer engaging a "child" in a discussion, but rather a developing young man or woman. It is certainly okay to be upfront and authentic with them. In fact, I truly believe teens appreciate authenticity more than they do adults who talk down to them or treat them like children. Even if your teen is immature or behind a few years emotionally, you can still model (by having a mature conversation with them) how adults relate or should relate. In some ways, you may feel that your teen is being treated like a child by you having to remove or lock up potentially dangerous items from your house. But you must keep in mind that when your teen's emotions are high, adults must step in to ensure safety. Until your teen can cope appropriately, you will have to take the assertive role.

You'll also want to learn about the various ways other teens have attempted to kill themselves. This will give you some idea of the types of things your teen may be thinking about. When I worked in a residential treatment facility some years ago, I learned about the various ways my young clients thought of killing themselves. They taught me a lot. Some kids were thinking of the following: running into traffic and playing it off as not paying attention, burning a charcoal grill in the garage or basement, turning a gun on themselves at a shooting range or while hunting with dad, causing a wreck while driving with a friend by pulling the steering wheel, getting restrained or pursued by police, and/or jumping out of a bedroom window. Some of the things these kids thought about were shocking, to say the least. They were heartbreaking as well.

Learning about the many ways teens think is significant to helping them. In fact, according to research, adolescent males tend to search for lethal weapons to assist in their suicide, while adolescent girls tend to engage in the act of overdosing. The use of firearms to assist in the suicide of both male and female adolescents is the leading cause of death in about 67% of suicides, according to the American Academy of Pediatrics Committee on Adolescence. More than 90% of suicides occur with firearms in this population. Most adults don't even know this fact. When I shared this statistic with an audience of parents at a conference they were quite shocked. There are many things parents and teachers need to know but have limited information about. In fact, research suggests that schools (and teachers) remain in the dark about adolescent suicide. Efforts are being made, at the state level, to educate and train schools and teachers about this epidemic. Sadly, many teachers lack the appropriate knowledge and training to counsel students struggling with suicidal thoughts. As a result, many refer students to outside clinics and agencies. Even more, parents also lack knowledge in this area which leads to most parents "winging it." Figuring out how and when to communicate with your teen is important to helping them get the help they need. It is important you learn how to provide a platform for smooth communication in order to then pursue the next step which is treatment. Following the pursuit of treatment, you will then need to decide whether or not you will involve your teen's school. It will be important that you, as my book will highlight, be strategic and authentic in communicating with the school. Because the educational system is often very detached from the mental health system, parents will have to serve as bridges between each system to help support their teen. Part of bridging this gap will include coordinating care with the school and your teen's mental health therapist. This may include obtaining the contact information of your teen's school psychologist/counselor and sharing that information with the outpatient therapist or psychiatrist. It may also include encouraging the school to reach out to your teen's therapist to ensure everyone is on the same page. You also need to consider if you will ask for supportive services such as an IEP (individualized education plan), 504 plan, or tutor to help with keeping your teen successful in school. Teens who are struggling with emotional challenges will often fall behind in school which could be an added or unnecessary stressor. Teens who are very competent and focused on their school success will benefit from the extra support until they are able to manage school and their suicidal thoughts better. Some teens may feel embarrassed by receiving these services. In cases such as this, your teen may benefit from learning more about these programs and understanding that each educational support can be temporary and will not follow them into their adult years.

Parents must realize that some school districts will not offer support unless they see a real need. Other schools may take a more passive approach to supporting a family, especially if the teen is already seeing a therapist outside of school. In cases such as these, you will need to rely on your teen's therapist for information on ways to pursue IEP's, 504 plans, cyber or home-schooling, or other forms of accommodations. Do go at this alone. In addition, once you learn of the state of your teen's mental health and educational needs, you will need to understand what treatment options are available to you. For example, some parents are unsure of when to pursue treatment for fear of overreacting, angering their teen, or creating stigma. This book will highlight ways you can discuss the need for treatment with your teen. I hope to encourage you and your teen to become your own advocate. Being humble during this process is important. You certainly don't want to approach anything involving this topic with an intellectualizing attitude. This can backfire. You would want to remain open to learning at all times, even if you've read almost every book on teen suicide. Teens can shock us. They have a way of telling us that we aren't as aware or insightful about them as we may think. You would also want to educate your teen during this process and ensure they understand what is really happening to them. Lack of knowledge can lead to failed attempts to heal oneself, discouragement, and confusion.

When parents encounter the world of mental health many feel they are walking in the dark all alone. Despite feeling heartbroken and possibly even confused, you must push forward. Pushing forward starts with self-knowledge. I hope you begin to see this book as a mini companion and an assistant to your self-paced learning experience. I will highlight the following in the pages ahead:

- Why teens turn to suicide.
- Thinking and behavioral patterns typical of suicidal teens.
- Risk and protective factors (i.e., things that create strengths and weaknesses).
- Examples of types of passive death wishes and direct suicidal statements.

- Information on hospitals and seeking help via 302 or 201, concrete tips on how schools (i.e., teachers, Principal's, or school counselors and psychologists) can help.

After writing my first book on mental health back in 2012-2013, I realized that hurting parents do not need a scientific book filled with psychobabble and research or statistical jargon. My hope is that this book will provide you with a practical resource

About this book

In chapter 1, I outline and explain definitions, concepts, challenges often faced when working with suicidal teens, and why this book is needed for parents and teachers.

In chapter 2, I focus on providing some explanation (based on research and my own clinical experience) of why adolescents turn to suicide. I will focus on the following potential causes: risk factors, untreated or poorly treated mental health conditions, trauma, failed experiences in psychotherapy, emotional and psychological challenges such as learned helplessness or apathy, low self-esteem, personality disorder traits, and the parent-child relationship. You will also learn about important signs that are displayed when a teen is contemplating suicide such as thinking errors, negative self-talk, an external or internal locus of control that leads to low self-esteem or feelings of helplessness, and negative attributions or perceptions.

In chapter 3 I will discuss concepts such as suicide-cluster, suicide-contagion, and collective-disturbance. I will also walk you through a trauma-informed approach to understanding what may lead to suicidal behaviors. This chapter aims to explain the influence that other teens and groups of teens can have on those considering suicide. A general view of other influences will also be examined.

In chapter 4, I will discuss where to start and what to do. I will outline various ways you can address suicidal teens and help them regain emotional and psychological stability. I will discuss and provide information on how to: acknowledge the problem correctly and begin a discussion, react empathically, and involve the teen's school. This chapter will include a case study to provide you with an example of a resistant and angry teen considering suicide. You will be provided with an example of how to address the teen with empathy as opposed to anger.

Chapter 5 will discuss different kinds of mental health providers as well as mental health treatment for suicidal teens. This chapter will walk you through typical treatment approaches for teens struggling with suicidal thoughts. I will discuss teens who struggle with varying degrees of suicidal thoughts and the different levels of treatment they would qualify for. Each case example provides an example of the level of care your teenager may qualify for. You will find examples of statements that should be avoided and can be harmful to teens who are suicidal. Language can make or break communication and can destroy self-esteem. Knowing what not to say is the first step toward ensuring your teen feels heard, supported, and safe. You will also find examples of questions you should ask during your teen's first appointment. The chapter will conclude with tips on how teachers can help. You are welcome to share this section with your teen's teacher with appropriate reference.

    Chapter 6 focuses on safety planning from a trauma-informed perspective. This chapter will focus on providing some knowledge on suicidal thoughts from a trauma-informed perspective. I will discuss the safety and crisis planning approach I often take with teens. I will briefly discuss debriefing and moving forward after a crisis. This chapter is for both you and your teen to learn how to design a practical safety/crisis plan that can be used at home and at school. Tips will be provided on how to structure the safety/crisis plan. I also provide an example of a trauma-focused activity that may help you and your teen build personal insight. You will find examples to help guide you. It is important I mention that I do not go into depth about trauma in this book. I do not discuss adoption, foster care, unexpected deaths, or any other traumatic events of this nature. However, we cannot overlook the impact of trauma on suicidal teens. There will be an example template as well. You will also find worksheets to practice concepts throughout chapters 5 and 6. It is my purpose in this book to highlight the importance of understanding and utilizing the best approaches to addressing the topic of suicide with your teen. Many of the tips and suggestions in this book have already been used by me in therapy with teens who are suicidal and with parents who are desperately looking for answers.

Chapter 7 will provide an overview of helping your teen stay in and maintain treatment, ways you can keep your teen's school informed or up-to-date, ways to stay connected to your teen's therapist, and barriers to treatment. You will learn about keeping treatment records and copies for future use. For example, I often encourage my clients and their parents to create a "therapeutic binder" that they can turn to when they need to be reminded of therapeutic activities completed, when the next appointment is, or where to find that school excuse slip signed by the therapist. When parents are emotionally overwhelmed it can be difficult to keep up with all of the forms, copies, appointments, etc. received during therapy. This chapter will include a brief list of ways you can stay organized.

Chapter 8 concludes with final points, concerns, and considerations. I also briefly discuss things I've learned about suicide over the years, personality disorders and suicidal behavior or thoughts, what to do when communication about suicide with a teen fails, facts for teachers about teen suicide, the role of teachers in preventing suicide and raising awareness, and ways to foster or maintain open communication with your teen.

Each chapter is constructed with the intent of providing you with enough information to feel informed, while also being careful not to overwhelm you with information. Each chapter aims to pique your interest and encourage you to do further research on your own. As I have stated multiple times in articles, blogs, and in my previous book, self-knowledge is powerful. Once you recognize that your teen needs help, it is to your advantage to research all you can and empower you and your family to care for itself.

Chapter 1

Why This Book Is Overdue For Parents and Teachers

"Sometimes things fall apart so better things can fall together."

- Marilyn Monroe

This book was written specifically to attract the attention of two of the most overlooked populations within the realm of mental health care which are parents (my primary audience) and teachers (my secondary audience). Research suggests that schools remain uninformed about ways to assist youths who are suicidal. They also remain uninformed about ways to reach out to families in need. As a result, the American Foundation for Suicide Prevention designed a "model policy" for middle and high school teachers interested in implementing a suicide prevention plan. The policy covers some of the same topics I cover in this book such as discussion of what causes suicidal behaviors, school-based supports, mental health services, and parent notification and involvement. These are important areas of concern for parents and teachers alike.

What the numbers are saying

According to the American Foundation for Suicide Prevention (2017), every single day there are about 121 suicides with 44,193 suicides per year. For adolescents between the ages of 15 – 24, suicide is the 2nd leading cause of death. In 2015, the suicide rate was about 12.5% for adolescents between ages 15 – 24. This age group is particularly vulnerable to suicidal ideation because of hormones and the limited development of higher order thinking and executive function in the frontal lobes. The frontal lobes are the "seat" of our personality development but also other important functions such as decision-making and impulse control. Because adolescent's lack the ability to make mature decisions and control their impulses they need adults who can understand how they are feeling and who are able to make the decisions they cannot make. Although I am not a neuro-scientist, I will focus briefly on how brain development or lack thereof influences suicidal ideations. It is important that parents and teachers focus on the biological influences of suicide.

We have an adolescent culture in today's world that has become desensitized to suicide due to an array of influences (some of which include art and music, social media, and pop psychology). We also have a society that continually fails to recognize teens of ethnic minority status who struggle with suicidal thinking. In fact, Native American Indians account for about the second highest rate of suicide (12.6), while Hispanics and Latinas/Latinos (5.8%), and African Americans (5.6%) show roughly similar rates but we rarely hear this. The American Association of Suicidology reports that in 2014, 2,224 African Americans's died by suicide in 2014 (1, 946 were males and 475 were females). Even more, although suicide occurs in many of the Native American tribes, it is an ever-present issue in the Jicarilla Apache Nation. Suicide among young American Indians nearly doubled the national rate in 2015. There is a need for parents and teachers to become further educated about the impact of suicide on teens of ethnic minority status and ways they can support them. Although the National Association of School Psychologists offer information on ways school counselors can work with youths from all cultural backgrounds, there are limited books written specifically to parents and teachers to empower them to work more effectively with teens of color. For Hispanic youths, The Suicide Prevention Resource Center reports that the acculturation process can trigger suicidal thoughts. A high level of perceived discrimination can also be associated with high risk for suicide in this population.

I've noticed that in the majority of cases school counselors and parents tend not to connect as often as they should on issues specific to youths of color. I'm hoping that we can bridge this gap. Teachers and parents need to become a team, especially in the lives of ethnic minority students who have become all too familiar with feeling left behind. We certainly need tools that can specifically address the significant issues facing ethnic minority youths who are suicidal.

After accepting an invitation in January 2017 to do a webinar on suicide from a national platform developed for teachers and parents, I recognized how little this population knew about teens who are contemplating suicide. I then began to receive emails and comments from parents asking me to do another webinar focused on what teachers and parents can do for needy teens. You can find that webinar by visiting simplek12.com and signing up for their membership. In the state of Pennsylvania, suicidal adolescents have become a "state

epidemic" in such a way that Pennsylvania's ACT 71 law was signed into law on June 26, 2014. It requires all school entities to:
- Adopt a youth suicide awareness and prevention policy
- Provide ongoing professional development and focus on providing useful clinical information to parents and mental health professionals
- Incorporate curriculum on this topic into a teacher's instructional programs

As a licensed therapist I am required, on a yearly basis, to engage in some form of suicide prevention training as a continuing education requirement. Suicide prevention and awareness for youngsters is a significant topic in today's society, primarily among parents, teachers, and mental health professionals.

What I believe most teens want

I strongly believe that teens want concrete and practical tools for minimizing the emotional, psychological, and sometimes physical pain they feel. Suicide, as you will see in the coming chapters, is often a way to cope with or decrease pain. It isn't an activity that all teens set out to engage in because "it's cool" or "interesting." It is a "way to heal" for most teens. As you know, most teens make drastic decisions often on impulse. When they feel overwhelmed with life their impulses tell them to end it all because "it would be better or easier." Most teens lack the executive functioning (a part of the frontal lobes behind the forehead that slowly develops and doesn't fully develop until about age 25) needed to make proper decisions, reach out for help, maturely process their emotions and thoughts, and avoid immediate gratification. For hurting teens immediate gratification is suicide. What's the point in living if living doesn't appeal to you? Some teens will do whatever they can to end it all. The pressure of school, social relationships, family, and management of their emotions and self-image can all be too much to cope with. Without the proper skills to manage emotions and reach out for help, suicide is often the last resort option. Some teens would rather end it all rather than reach out for help and ruin their identity and image.

What parents need

Parents are often looking for unique approaches to address the topic of teen suicide and ultimately encourage psychotherapy. Parents often have to learn by trial and error what services are available and determine the best approach to finding a good therapist. I provide example case studies to help you understand how a trained therapist might approach a teenager about suicide. This will give you some practice on how you may be able to broach the topic with your teen. I also provide example case studies of behaviors that would qualify for various levels of care. For example, teens who are suicidal but have not acted on their thoughts would not qualify for admission to a hospital or a residential program. Teens like this would most likely benefit from outpatient therapy. The case studies outline varying degrees of suicidal thoughts and behaviors. You will also find an outline of a safety plan that you can use with your teen to help them document their challenges and ways to cope. A safety plan is a great way to put in writing daily challenges, triggers, and ways to cope.

In the following pages we will explore some ways you may approach your teen about your concerns and pursuing treatment. I've learned that many parents want tips on how to maintain open communication and stay organized throughout the entire process of pursuing treatment, maintaining treatment, and terminating treatment. Most parents don't realize that they need to build their knowledge and skill in a step-by-step fashion. Not in a rushed manner that can lead to burn-out. I encourage you to do a lot of pacing while reading this book.

This guidebook was written for you, the parent, who is feeling uncertain, alone, and confused about this topic. Great effort has been made to provide you with updated and empirical information on research, counseling approaches, and trauma-informed tools. You will learn a little bit about trauma-informed approaches that I have used to treat suicidal youths, especially youths with a complicated or traumatic family history. Adolescents who have experienced a traumatic situation tend to lack the ability to trust and engage which leads to avoidance of psychotherapy or other forms of support and unhealthy coping skills. It has been my experience with parents that they are in constant search of new ways to support their teen. I'm sure you can relate. So with my background and training in child and adolescent care, this book will offer some techniques from CBT (Cognitive Behavior Therapy) including trauma-informed care that you can use. The techniques discussed will focus on evaluating thoughts, feelings, and behavior including the influence of trauma (if applicable).

Trauma-informed topics that will be briefly mention the influence of risk and protective factors, circumstances that can trigger suicidal thoughts, the influence of trauma on the brain, the development of mental health challenges that lead to suicidal thoughts, and differentiating between typical therapy and trauma therapy.

Thankfully, there is an expanding empirical literature base that supports the use of trauma-informed techniques with teens who are considered "high risk" or a danger to themselves or others. Suicidal teens, especially those who have attempted suicide more than once, qualify as "high risk." Tools used for "high risk" youths include but are not limited to:
- Crisis and safety plans,
- Frequent review of treatment plans developed in counseling,
- Incorporation of assessment measures to identify weaknesses, strengths, or needs,
- Education on mindfulness, guided imagery, and relaxation techniques,
- Teaching on the importance of recognizing

hyperarousal, emotional reactivity, irritability, and depression, and

It has been my experience that parents and teachers both appreciate therapists who will go the extra mile to support them. They appreciate the therapist who has the teen's best interest at heart, takes time with them to explain things, offers suggestions or advice, and/or refers them to other people who can provide insight.

My hope is that with this book you will feel empowered to engage in self-knowledge and advocate for yourself and your teen. As Maya Angelou said "do the best you can until you know better. Then, when you know better, do better." Sometimes the only remedy for a teen who is feeling suicidal is to show them that you care.

NOTES

Chapter 2

Why Some Teens Turn To Suicide

When a flower doesn't bloom, you fix the environment in which it grows, not the flower.

-Alexender Den Heijer

On average, every 2 weeks, someone jumps from San Fransisco's 4,200 foot long Golden Gate Bridge. The Golden Gate Bridge is considered to be the "prime location" for carrying out a suicide. The bridge not only sits high above the waters and is 4,200 feet long, but is also known to have "assisted" in the suicide of at least 3,000 or more people, according to research. This is a terrifying reality. It's a shock that 3,000+ people wanted to die. This high number staggers me each time I look at it.

When I counsel parents of teens contemplating suicide I often encourage them to look at some of the statistics and facts on suicide. The numbers have a way of waking us to the need around us. When you take a moment to look at the staggering numbers, the conceptualization of suicide as part of an "illness" becomes more clearly understood. If you don't look at the numbers you will likely continue to be unmoved by and confused about why so many people would want to take their own life. When parents find out that their teen is suicidal their first thought may be "why?" It is important that you learn more about what it is that your teen wants or is crying out for by displaying suicidal behaviors and maintaining thoughts of suicide. The first step toward understanding teen suicide is to read about the topic, educate yourself, open your mind to the various reasons why, and embrace some of the general facts about the topic. I encourage you to start out by researching adult suicide and then moving to teen suicide. This provides the foundational knowledge to help you understand the major impact of suicide on the adolescent population. I suggest you learn as much as you can. Having this knowledge will ensure you are prepared to not only advocate for your teen and have full conversations with them about it but also have the tools to help them cope appropriately.

When I began counseling suicidal teens in a teaching university/hospital for my year-long internship, I found myself almost completely uneducated about many of the teens I saw and their suicidal thoughts. I recognized that I had not been exposed to the nature of teen suicide, the many reasons for teens hiding them, and their various treatment needs. It took years of counseling experience, the pursuit of self-knowledge, and conversations with families to help me understand this topic better. With counseling experience and career maturity I was able to delve deeper into the needs of my teen clients and figure out what parents (as well as teachers) were in need of. About 9 years later, this awareness and knowledge led to a partnership with Simplek12.com (a website dedicated to the advancement of educators) who asked me to provide trainings on the topic of suicide.

This was a great first step in advocating for needy teens. But we still need more in-depth information about suicide to be made available to laymen, parents, and teachers. We also need more mainstream coverage focusing on teen suicide such as major news stations, daily newspapers, talk-radio, and podcasts. Until then, the topic of teen suicide will remain largely unavailable to those who do not directly search for it. As a result, I encourage you to reach out to your local newspaper, talk-radio, blogs, and other sources of media and request that more guests be interviewed about the topic of teen suicide. Draw attention and encourage your community to embrace it so that more people will become knowledgeable about it. Starting a conversation is the most important step of the process.

Some reasons why teens turn to suicide

Teens consider suicide for a variety of reasons but some common reasons are:

- Challenges with peer groups such as being bullied, being ousted or ignored, or feeling left out or disliked.
- Challenges with keeping up in school academically.
- Poor or no connection with teachers or other adults within the school.
- Challenges with home-life such as divorce, difficulties within the parent-child relationship, frequent moving from location to location, domestic violence, trauma, abuse, or neglect, untreated or poorly treated parental mental health, moderate to severe sibling rivalry, death, etc.
- Depression, anxiety, or other mental health

conditions.
- Low self-esteem, self-efficacy, and self-worth.
- Untreated or poorly treated medical conditions such as diabetes, heart conditions, or obesity.

There are endless reasons why teens often resort to suicide as a remedy to their problems. But over the past few years as a child and adolescent therapist, I have noticed that there are typically three major reasons why parents reach out to me to counsel their teen:

- The teen is being bullied and as a result is struggling with mental health, self-esteem, or finding a positive peer group.
- Domestic violence, trauma, abuse, or some other major family event that has resulted in a change of behavior, emotions, or mindset.
- The teen is unable to cope with depression, anxiety, cutting, or suicidal thoughts.

Even though teens are different from each other, you can sometimes find similarities in their reasons for wanting to die. We must also remember that teens who have been in foster care, adopted, or in multiple residential treatment facilities may struggle with thoughts of suicide. Can you imagine how you would feel as a youth placed in foster care (being sent to a variety of homes and possibly rejected by many). Can you imagine living in a residential facility (where you have to be taken care of by strangers you don't have a bond with)? It can be traumatizing, to say the least. That's why in many cases, foster and adoptive parents must be educated through parenting classes or other necessary trainings before the foster or adoption process begins. These kids struggle with a lot and may be at risk for future mental health problems and suicidal thoughts.

Passive-death wishes and direct suicide statements

One of the best parts of my community conferences, presentations, and webinars is when the audience participates and begins asking tough questions such as "what are the signs of suicide?" "what should I be looking for in a teen who has attempted suicide before?" These questions are often the beginning of a great educational experience. It is typically during these moments that I realize the great need for this topic. I once had a teacher ask during the question and answers portion of one of my presentations "do teens show the same signs of wanting to kill themselves or do they show different signs? As you probably know, teens can be very difficult to read. Although we cannot be certain as to why some teens turn to suicide, there are often a few common reasons why. A typical reason I hear from teens is "I don't feel heard" or "I feel disrespected." In order to be "heard" teens often use passive death wishes or indirect messages to express their thoughts and feelings. For these teens, I truly believe they are using suicidal language to achieve three things:

- Get their immediate need for attention and affection met.
- To test others to see if they are truly as concerned as they say they are.
- To get a point across, whatever that may be.

Passive-death wishes can range from mild to severe. A passive-death wish is a statement about suicide that is made indirectly. A few examples of passive-death wishes include but are not limited to:

- "I wonder what would happen if I were not living on this earth."
- "Would you miss me if I killed myself?"
- "I wonder what heaven or hell is like?"
- "I really want to be with grandma again."
- "I wonder if I could get out of school if I killed myself. Then I wouldn't have to deal with the bullying."

- "Classes are too frustrating and hard. I don't want to live here anymore."

Aside from passive-death wishes are direct death statements. These statements are powerful as many teens express their desire, their knowledge of what to do, and their plan. Direct suicidal threats/statements include but are not limited to:
- "I'm going to kill myself at the first chance I have."
- "Life is not worth all of this at all. I'm going to change my fate."
- "Why should I live? What will I gain? I just want to die. I have a plan and I'm not telling you."
- "I will kill myself but you'll never know when or how."

These kinds of suicidal statements may be considered threats. When these statements are made, as a parent, you have the right to hospitalize your teen (if they are under the age of 14). If your teen is over age 14, you will have to either convince your teen to go to the hospital to sign themselves in (learn more in chapter 5) or you can hospitalize them against their will. If you decide to go with hospitalizing your teen against their will, I really

Page 46

encourage you to consider the pros and cons of this decision. There is a long list of pros and cons. Some of the benefits of hospitalizing your teen against his or her will may include: getting an immediate evaluation, receiving instant medication management by the attending physician, and 24/7 supervision from staff and the doctor. The cons may include: your teen having a mental health record of being hospitalized, getting angry with you about forcing the issue and having to be accompanied to the hospital by police and an ambulance if you hospitalize them against their will. The process of hospitalizing your teen against his or her will can be traumatizing and de-stabilizing. You will want to weigh whether this is necessary and worth the possible end result. You should also keep in mind that even if you attempt to get your teen hospitalized against his or her will, the hospital may not see a reason to follow through and can then release the teen. This entire process can create tension between you and your teen as well as a sense of defeat on your part. The entire process can be humiliating, embarrassing, and time-consuming. In some cases, the hospital may not even have an available bed for your teen. You can certainly call ahead of time to the hospital you would want your teen to be admitted to see if they have bed availability. Some hospitals will provide this information and others will not.

If you must make this decision to keep your teen safe, trust your intuition and be ready to face anger and resentment from your teen. They may be angry but you must stand firm in your decision. Try your hardest not to display uncertainty and fear of your teen's reactions. Explain, repeatedly, your intent to help and support them. Again, trust your intuition, seek guidance from someone who will tell you the truth, weigh the pros and cons, and proceed with caution. You also want to be sure not to overthink the decision as well or you will find yourself in limbo.

Typical behavioral patterns of suicidal teens

Sometimes teens act out more when they are feeling suicidal or thinking about suicide. Some teens, as you probably already know, are too immature or afraid to reveal their thoughts so they act out. When teens act out behaviorally, it can be difficult to believe they are suffering emotionally because of the aggressiveness or inappropriateness of their behavior. Boys and girls display their emotions differently, as you know. In fact, research suggests that males tend to use more aggressive means to complete a suicide (such as using weapons or guns), while girls use less aggressive means such as pills or cutting. Girls may not act out behaviorally at all times like boys might. Girls may act out but in different ways which causes them to be overlooked by adults. Falling through the cracks is easy when you're a girl who seems calm and in control all of the time. But girls will often try to meet their emotional needs when they are suicidal such as by drinking or using pills, dating multiple boys or trying to get attention of a sexual nature, being intimate with multiple boys, or developing a negative reputation. Some girls also become bullies, manipulative, or calculating. Teen girls with borderline personality traits may begin to display very poor boundaries, sexualized behaviors, unstable relationship patterns, and cutting or other forms of self-injury. Males may begin to use drugs, act out oppositionally, refuse to complete school work, skip school, hang out with the wrong crowds, enter into gangs or unhealthy peer groups, or develop a fascination with weapons.

Typical behaviors of teens who are suicidal include but are not limited to:

- Isolating, withdrawing, hiding.
- Depressed or anxious mood or affect.
- Acting like "they don't care."
- Falling behind in grades.
- Combative, argumentative, or irritable.
- Labile or changing moods.
- Neglecting to take medications or see a therapist.
- Experimenting with or engaging in cutting or other forms of self-harm. I want to emphasize that not all teens who cut or engage in self-harm want to die but some do.
- Seeming to avoid conversation, eye contact, or help/support from others.
- Losing motivation, hope, or interest in life.
- Sharing suicidal thoughts or plans with peers and pressuring them not to tell.
- Taking weapons to school, carrying them or hiding them.
- Preoccupation with death or dying.
- A major change in personality, dress, or attitude.
- Goth or gange-related behaviors, interests, or idealization.

It is important to keep in mind that these behaviors alone do not always indicate that a teen is considering suicide. But what it does indicate is that something is going on that needs addressing. I encourage you, as the parent, to watch out for these behaviors and see if you can connect the dots between their behaviors, comments, and performance in school and everyday life. This is important data for you if you ever decide to pursue a therapist or speak with the school about your concerns. I do encourage you to reach out to your teen's teacher and ask if they have noticed any of the above behaviors, especially if you have.

Things to keep in mind

It is sad to say that many teens in today's society feel discouraged by the challenges they are facing such as bullying, social pressures, growing up in a society that seems to have become vain and callous, getting and maintaining good grades, deciding on higher education and a career path, pleasing adults, staying out of trouble, and dating violence and abuse. Other teens are facing severe mental illness such as psychotic disorders, bipolar disorder, and severe depression. In addition to this, some teens have to face their traumatic histories and try to separate what has happened to them from who they are becoming. Teens today face a lot and adults remain in the dark because everything that happens, mostly happens online. In other cases, teens can be really good at hiding their true selves.

Some teens are highly influenced by their "separate identity" online and may be experiencing a whole new world. Bullying, particularly cyber bullying, tends to occur online and many teens have taken their lives as a result. Teens can feel isolated from supportive people in their worlds. As if this wasn't enough, embarrassment, shame, and guilt may hold teens hostage from reaching out to the adults in their lives. Does this sound like your teen? If so, you'll want to keep in mind two important categories if you suspect your teen may be considering suicide. These categories includ thought patterns and behavioral patterns.

Typical thought patterns of suicidal teens

Thought patterns are often the culprit for triggering suicidal ideation and suicide-contagion (a concept to be further discussed in chapter 3). Thinking errors, or cognitive distortions, are skewed perceptions based on little fact and much emotion. For example, let's say that you had a very bad night in which you only slept for 3 hours. You wake up in the morning and are greeted by your mother who says you look tired and could use more sleep. Instead of taking this statement as a show of love from a supportive mother, you take the comment as an insult on how you look. This could be labeled as black and white thinking, generalization, or mind-reading. Here are a few common thinking errors that I teach my teen clients to watch out for in themselves:

- **Black and white thinking** is also known as polarized thinking. This thinking pattern is often displayed when an individual is unwilling to (or cannot) look at a situation from various angles. Thinking is narrow, short-sighted, and almost always immature. There is no "gray" thinking for this individual. It is black or white only.
- **Generalization** is a pattern of thinking in which a person takes one situation (good or bad) and generalizes what happened to other situations in one's life. For example, let's say your teen daughter goes to prom and gets made fun of because of a hole in her dress. She feels humiliated and calls you in a panic asking you to pick her up. She concludes that she will never be able to face her school again and vows to avoid walking during graduation for fear of getting another hole in her

graduation gown.
- **Mind-reading** can be just as bad as the two thought patterns above. Mind-readers believe they are able to "read the mind" of other people or predict what will happen. Most teens are entrapped by mind-reading and by assuming they know what others are thinking them. Some teens will also say things like "what's the point in going? I'm just going to fail anyways."

Thinking errors are important to discuss with your teen. Thinking errors tend to be the foundation of the challenges many of my teen clients face before they ever consider suicide. Once they become exhausted by their thinking errors, they then consider suicide as a remedy to their problems. It is often after a few therapy sessions that thinking errors become exposed. The sad part is that thinking errors are difficult to identify by parents and even more difficult to help teens understand. A therapist is often able to help teens see the benefit in identifying skewed perceptions better than parents can. The therapist's authority and the nature of the relationship can cause teens to accept their viewpoint better.

Aside from the above thinking errors are teen thoughts revolving around:

- **Nihilistic thinking:** "The world is ending" thought pattern is typical of teens. But teens who are feeling suicidal and having suicidal ideations may engage in this type of thinking that causes them to feel even more hopeless or helpless. Teens with borderline personality traits may exhibit this type of thinking style. Teens exhibiting nihilistic thought patterns are almost always suicidal because they are depressed and uncertain of their future. Nothing can help. There is no reason to pursue help. There is no ultimate purpose.
- **Existential questioning:** This type of thinking may be exhibited as "why am I here?" "I want out of here." "Life is so very hard and I don't like it." Although these thoughts are normal thoughts that many of us think at some point in our lives, teens who constantly have these thoughts are at risk for suicidal ideation. Existential questioning is a term I "created" and use with teens who are questioning life and the challenges of life. Too many questions with little answers can lead to

depression and ultimately, suicidal thoughts.
- **Delusional beliefs:** Delusional beliefs are beliefs that have no logical or correct foundation and are based on skewed, illogical beliefs that are triggered by emotion. A delusion is a strong conviction that is held by an individual despite evidence to the contrary. It is not a strong constitution or even faith. It is a belief based on little no evidence and may be bizzare or non-bizarre. A bizarre delusional thought is that your teen has been "chosen" by aliens to be their leader and that your teen is waiting for the spaceship to come and get them. A non-bizarre delusional thought pattern may involve your teen strongly believing they are being harassed, stalked, and watched by another peer online. Because many teens are bullied in today's world and tend to be bullied online, this delusional thought is non-bizarre, but still poses a challenge because it isn't true. Teens who have delusional thoughts are at risk for suicidal ideation due to feeling all alone, isolated, and unbelieved by others.
- **Negative self-talk:** Self-talk can be defined as conversations we have with ourselves about an event occurring in our lives. Teens have a lot of

negative self-talk because of their fragile and under-developed sense of self. When self-talk is negative, depressive thoughts are also likely to occur because the negative self-talk almost always involves talking about one's capabilities or challenges. For example, your teen may have negative self-talk around their ability to make friends. They may say things to themselves such as: "you aren't good enough to make and keep friends," "you are so boring that no one will ever want to talk to you," or "you'll never find a girlfriend." These thoughts are often pre-requisites for depression and suicidal ideation.

- **Questioning one's faith or religion:** Questioning faith is something I truly believe most of us go through at some point in our lives. Teens go through this a lot because they begin to ask the tough questions about life, existence, and meaning. Many teens have engaged me in conversation about the reason for everything humans do on a daily basis. These questions call on me to rely on my faith and my existential/philosophical background to answer in a genuine fashion. For me, I tell my teens the truth by explaining the natural and raw experience of questioning all of life. For teens who are suicidal, questioning faith is something you are likely to see. However, questioning one's faith doesn't mean that the teen is thinking about suicide of course. But I think it's important for you to ask your teen why they seem to be struggling with questions. The conversation should be free of religious talk (i.e., traditional religiosity that includes an element of guilt-tripping and manipulation), threats or anger, and judgment. I've learned over the years the importance of approaching teens carefully when they are questioning their faith. One wrong move, statement, or question could lead them to reject the faith completely, turn to destructive means of pacifying their confusion, and/or completely reject you as their parent.

Teens who are struggling with suicidal thoughts need to be able to express their thoughts to the adults in their lives. We can assure teens that we are available to them by simply listening and avoiding trying to fix their problems. I've learned in many sessions with teens that they only want to be heard and understood. Not fixed. The minute we start to come across as if we are trying to "fix them," we lose them. As a parent, being aware of the above thinking patterns will help you identify what your teen is needing emotionally and psychologically. You can use the concepts in this chapter and all throughout the book to help guide your communication with your teen.

Activity on identifying thinking errors

Below you will find examples of teens who are experiencing cognitive distortions (the above thought patterns. You can read the scenario below and answer the question below to test your knowledge and practice. Answers are provided at the end of the chapter.

Thinking error #1: Lizzie is a 14-year-old teen who lives with her father and visits with her mother every week. She attends Ligonier High School and is in the 10th grade. She gets all A's and B's but will occasionally get a D. She started dating a young man who is on a very popular basketball team in the local area. She really likes him and struggles with feelings of jealousy that other girls may like and take him away. Lizzie's father decides to broach the topic and ask why she has been so emotionally distant lately. Lizzie's father finds out that she is not only struggling with jealousy but feelings of rejection (even though Lizzie's boyfriend isn't rejecting her at all). Lizzie reports to her father that there are no signs of her boyfriend rejecting her but that she still feels he does. Lizzie provides her father with an example of what has made her feel so paranoid. She reports that her previous boyfriend seemed happy but was plotting a day and time to break up with her. Although her father can understand the complexity of teen love, he believes that Lizzie's thinking isn't 100% correct.

What thinking error(s) do you think may be occurring here? What could contribute to that thinking error? What is another way Lizzie could look at the situation? Write your answer below:

Thinking error #2: Jacob is an all-star player on his school's basketball team. He is 15 years old and has attended Lake View High school for about 2 years after his parents moved from their previous home. He gets straight A's and has never been suspended. However, after his grandmother unexpectedly became ill and was rushed to the hospital, Jacob hasn't wanted to talk to anyone including his grandmother. He believes that she will die even though the doctors tell him she has a 90% chance of living. His grandmother had a mini-stroke but was able to get to the hospital in enough time for the doctors to intervene. Although his grandmother was laughing and verbose for the first time in 3 days, Jacob still could not shake the feeling that his grandmother may die. He cried at the thought of it after getting into bed to sleep. His mind races every single night and he can't help but call or text his grandfather every few hours to check on her. He is now asking questions about life and why these things have to happen. He is very angry and refuses to pray or attend church.

What thinking error(s) do you think may be occurring here? How might you address this situation as his parent? Write your answer below:
_____

Thinking error #3: Nekiya is a 13-year-old African American teen who was "diagnosed" as gifted by her school. She struggles in class the majority of the time due to boredom and wanting to do her own thing such as read or study a project. Her teachers reported to both of her parents that she seems oppositional anytime someone tries to redirect her attention off of preferred activities in school. Both parents including Nekiya were invited to the school for a meeting with the Principal.

Nekiya reported to the Principal that she is constantly thinking of more interesting things to do and that she doesn't mean to be rude to her teachers. She reported feeling inadequate when engaging with other kids her age. She reported "I don't think anyone likes me. They didn't like me at my previous school and they don't like me now. Why would they?" Nekiya's parents jumped into the conversation to reassure her of her positive qualities, but she didn't believe them. She replied, "thanks, mom and dad but you're only saying that because I'm your child." When her Principal began to outline all of her accomplishments and good grades she replied "yeah but you're my Principal and are paid to say nice things. I don't believe I'll ever be good at anything so why listen in school? It's over for me. I would rather be dead."

What thinking error(s) do you think may be occurring here and why? How would you address Nekiya about this way of thinking?

Thinking error #4: Beckah is a 17-year-old biracial female who has been home-schooled for the majority of her life. Her parents decided to home-school her when she began to struggle with peers bullying her. Her parents placed her in almost every extracurricular activity available to her within the community. She was great in every extracurricular activity she signed up for. Now that Beckah was ready to go off to college and fly solo, she began to experience anxiety over leaving her family home and becoming an independent adult. Not only was she suffering from thinking negative things about herself and her abilities, but she also began to believe that the college she was accepted to was watching her every move. At bedtime, she would take blankets out of her closet and hang them over her bedroom window for fear that the President of her college was watching her sleep. One night her parents found her sleeping on the floor and her window curtains drawn closed. They asked, "what is going on Beckah?" She replied, "my college is watching everything I do because they want to make sure they chose the right person for their program." Beckah's parents reported to me during a family session that they were highly concerned about Beckah's state of mind and felt that she was paranoid. As her therapist, I remember explaining paranoia to her family and encouraging them to "track" the date and time including the content of her paranoid thoughts. Her thoughts eventually resulted in an admission, against her will, to a hospital because of a suicide attempt. She reported her suicide attempt to be the result of her believing "with all of my heart and mind that I am not good enough for my college."

What thinking error(s) do you think may be occurring here? Write your answer below: Could Beckah be struggling with more than one thought pattern? If yes, what type of thought pattern and why?

_____
_____
_____
_____
_____
_____
_____
_____
_____
_____
_____
_____
_____

It is important that I add that not all "thinking errors" are errors. In some cases, there may be an element of truth in these thoughts but the problem is that fear and anxiety tend to skew these thoughts. When teens begin to struggle with more than one thought pattern, it is important to explore why and then consider counseling. Some teens get so caught up in their fears that they don't realize their thinking patterns are unhealthy, one-sided, and self-destructive.

Suicidal Ideations with or without a plan

It is important to know if your teen has a plan that accompanies their suicidal thoughts. I tend to receive a lot of questions from parents, teachers, and other therapists about teen suicide plans. A typical question I get is often "when do I call the hospital or tell someone else that my teen needs help?" It is saddening to see just how uncertain many of the adults are about what steps to take once a teen reveals suicidal thoughts. I can't blame any of them for feeling confused or uncertain. Teens are often very skilled at keeping things from adults. It can seem as if your teen is always a million miles ahead of you. But this should not be an excuse for why you cannot figure out if your teen has a suicide plan. You can often find out by doing a little research with peers, teachers, or looking in their room. Although I often discourage an invasion of privacy, this is a crisis and your teen's safety is at risk.

You should always look for traces of a suicide plan. If your teen has a plan (i.e., a plan that is well thought out, detailed, and methodical), immediate intervention is needed. Teens who have a suicide plan have thought about it extensively and have most likely weighed the pros and cons of killing themselves. A teen who does not have a suicide plan may not be as lethal as the teen who does, but he/she still deserves immediate attention. When teens think about suicide they are trying to figure out how to either internalize their emotions or get rid of them completely. They may be incapable of emotion regulation and may feel trapped, hopeless, or helpless. Teens who have suicidal thoughts should be asked if they have ever thought of how they would kill themselves. If you don't feel comfortable doing this, you can certainly reach out to a trusted teacher, a close relative, or a therapist and ask them to poke around for this information. Some teens are so methodical, mature, and smart that they will tell you they don't have a plan so that you can't thwart their plan. If you suspect this, I encourage you to involve someone else in getting this information from the teen. You should also put potentially dangerous items away or lock them up. Items that can be potentially dangerous include but is not limited to:

- Knives (hunting, cooking, etc)
- Any weapons in the house or keys to the gun cabinet
- Car keys that can be stolen
- Medications in the medicine cabinet or kitchen
- Vitamins that can be overdosed on
- Ropes, ties, chains, or strings
- Lighters or matches
- Beauty tools such as tweezers, hair scissors, etc.
- Pencil sharpeners, staples, or other similar objects

You might be looking at this list wondering how you are going to protect your teen from every potentially dangerous item there is, especially in your home and at school. But the goal is not to protect your teen from these things but rather set the tone that safety is important while they are having suicidal thoughts. These items don't have to be locked up or put away forever. You are simply removing these things from your teen's sight in hopes of removing them from your teen's mind until they are able to cope in other ways.

You will also want to consider the extent of the suicide plan and the intensity of your teen's thoughts. For example, you can use a scaling question such as "on a scale from 1 - 10 (1 being very bad, 10 being very good) where are your thoughts?" You can also ask your teen to help you understand what triggered the suicidal thoughts. In many cases, teens can have suicidal thoughts and intent to act but have not a clue as to how they are going to carry it out. These teens are easier to work with because they are too afraid, confused, or uncertain to carry out their plan. But never let this cause you to assume everything is okay. You always want to be alert and prepared with a teen who has suicidal thoughts, despite the level of intensity of the thoughts.

Direct threat <u>without</u> a plan

A direct threat is a statement that expresses a desire to carrying out a suicidal thought but with no real way of carrying it out. For example, a teen may say something like this: "I am really ready to die. There's no point in living in this world. I want to die tonight. I just don't know what I'm going to do yet." A teen who expresses intent to die with a direct threat but with no plan can sometimes be convinced that their suicidal thoughts are not the best way to cope. Teens who do not have a plan have not fully processed their suicidal thoughts. They may have a strong desire but no real or logical plan. You still want to keep an eye on a teen who is at this level. Just because they don't have a plan doesn't mean they will never figure it out. Some teens need the right time to figure things out and then they act on their intent.

Direct threat <u>with</u> a plan

A direct threat is similar to the one above but with a plan. A teen may say something like this: "I'm really ready to die. There's no point in living in this world. I want to die tonight. I'm going to take my grandfather's bottle of pills, go to sleep, and wake up in heaven." This is not only a threat but a threat with high intent. When your teen expresses a threat, has a high level of intent (or a made up mind), and a plan you want to act immediately. You want to either get crisis support involved or take your teen to the nearest hospital for a psychiatric evaluation. You should also inform the school (a teacher, a counselor, the Principal, etc) of your teen's threat, intent, and means to carry it all out. Once you learn that your teen has a thought, high intent, and a plan you'll want to clean your house of any items (such as the ones listed above) that can be used to assist them in carrying out a suicide. You want to make it as difficult as possible for them to find things to harm themselves with. If your teen is very intent on killing themselves you may also want to consider calling your local crisis hotline, calling the police, and then having your child taken to the hospital. There are many drawbacks to having the police take your teen to the hospital so you will want to consider the pros and cons beforehand. When the police are called to get involved in a situation of a teen who is 14 or older, your teen will acquire a criminal record and will be admitted to the hospital against their will. This, as you will learn more of in chapter 5, is a 302 or involuntary admission to a hospital. You will only want to use this route if your teen is refusing to receive treatment, is a real danger to self or others, and will not at least get into the car to go to the hospital for an evaluation. It is my belief that a 302 for an adult, age 18 or older, is much worse than a record for a teen under the age of 18 years old. As an adult, once a 302 is issued it will be difficult for that adult to purchase a gun in the United States. There may also be further charges or legal barriers encountered as a result of the 302. For teens, the record will not follow them into adulthood. Either way, informing your teen of their options and the consequences may be enough to force them to go to the hospital on their own.

Keeping track of what's happening

All suicide threats (with or without a plan) must be taken seriously. Teachers who learn of suicidal thoughts should document their concerns and any conversations they have had with a teen or the teen's family. You, as the parent, can suggest the teacher document communication with your teen in case something happens where authorities or mental health providers may benefit from that information. You should also document the date, time, and content of discussions had with your teen's teacher or school. Keeping a record of when things happen and what was said will help you down the road. All suicidal threats or statements should be discussed at great length (even if your teen refuses to digest what you say). If you can get your teen talking, that's wonderful. If not, that's okay too. You cannot force them. That will backfire. You want to give your teen time to open up about this issue. It can be embarrassing and many teens would rather not process the topic with a parent. That's okay. Perhaps they aren't mature enough to talk as maybe you would like them to be. Give them time. You can give them space while also keeping your eyes open. To help prevent follow through of a suicide plan it is important to reach out to your local crisis hotline.

If you are in the Pittsburgh area of Pennsylvania, I encourage you to reach out to ReSolve Crisis Network at 1-888-796-8226. You can also contact this number in the event you believe a 302 (discussed further in chapter 5) is necessary to keep your teen safe. For all other crises across the nation, you can contact the Suicide Lifeline at 1-800-273-8255 or visit their website at http://www.suicidepreventionlifeline.org.

What we all should know about teens considering suicide

I've learned, over the course of my career, the importance of trying to understand and nurture those who struggle with suicidal thoughts as opposed to shutting them down, minimizing their thoughts, and making them feel "abnormal" for having them. I learned during the first 2-3 years in my field why shutting down or minimizing the experience of someone with suicidal thoughts can not only lead them to complete suicide, but also have a reason to do it. It is a missed opportunity to understand life through their eyes. As a result, I have listed some of the things I learned about teens who think about, consider, and attempt suicide:

- **Most teens want to talk about suicide:** When seeing clients for the first time, I often ask (as part of my intake) if they have ever thought of suicide or attempted suicide. I ask the question very nonchalantly in order to dispel myths, reduce defensiveness, and model openness about the topic. If a client tells me they have considered suicide I ask if they have shared their thoughts with others. Many of my clients tell me they have kept their thoughts of suicide secret because they feared backlash, judgment, or minimization of their feelings. I have learned over time that many of my adolescent clients, and some of the adults I see, want to talk about suicide but fear others will see them as "depressing" or "pessimistic."

- **Just because a teen thinks of suicide doesn't mean**

they truly want to die: For individuals who have thoughts of suicide for long periods of time and who may have attempted to take their own lives, may be conflicted about the entire thing. Suicide is often something that is considered after years of suffering, after multiple attempts to pursue therapy and heal, and after multiple traumatic or emotionally upsetting events. Suicide is like a "band-aid" for some people. Sadly, these teens fail to realize that this "band-aid" is not going to solve anything. It will hurt more than expected. Teens also struggle to understand that multiple people will hurt at their loss. This temporary band-aid is not going to fix it. I truly believe teens who struggle with suicidal thoughts know this deep down inside but are too distracted by searching for something to end their pain.

- **Self-injurious behaviors do not always mean a teen wants to die:** Non-suicidal self-injury includes cutting, burning, or harming self in some fashion without the intent of causing permanent damage or death. Some teens report harming themselves so badly that they needed to go to the hospital for medical treatment but did not want to die. Some youths are flirting with the idea of death and dying when they self-harm, while others are not. In very severe cases of self-injury, the teen often comes very close to death but is able to live due to medical intervention or the intervention of family members. Youths who play the "choking game" almost always come close to death. The choking game (or the "fainting game" as some kids call it) is a game in which kids chock each other or themselves until they are unable to breathe. The goal is to induce temporary unconsciousness. Some kids find this state of unconsciousness pleasurable. Other teens with severe self-destructive behaviors feel the need to severely self-harm with knives and other pointed objects to let go of "painful emotions." When I worked at a teaching university seeing fire-setters and teens who had severe self-injurious marks all over their body, I realized that many of these kids did not necessarily want to die. They wanted to "stop" the pain and the only way they knew how (without causing irrevocable damage) was to create situations that would inflict some kind of physical pain on themselves. I had a 10-year-old fire-setter who could not be left alone with his grandmother because he would run off and find something in the house to catch on fire. He ended up burning down the family home. He then began to cut and burn himself. I later found out, after 90 days of working with him, that he did not want to die but rather stop the rumination that he had suffered from for years following a sexual assault.

- **If an teen has one scary suicide attempt it may mean they will try it again at a later time:** Research suggests that when someone has attempted suicide (even 1 attempt) future attempts are more likely to occur. It's as if the 1st suicide attempt makes the individual less afraid of committing the next. My experience has been that a 1st suicide attempt may be like a "test round" to see what would happen. Teens typically take this approach. Another view of this is that individuals who attempt suicide may be more aggressive in the future with their 2nd attempt now that they understand how the process goes.

- **Having suicidal thoughts does not automatically mean the teen needs "help:"** Society believes that if an individual is having thoughts or questions about suicide that they must need psychiatric treatment. I want to dispel this myth today. Suicide is as much a part of life as other human challenges and teens will have questions about it. That's normal. It should be expected. Questions, curiosity, or interest should not be taboo or pathologized. Acting on suicidal thoughts or researching the topic in order to eventually kill oneself is the real problem. If a teen mentions it, questions it, or seems to be exploring it, it is okay to ask them why but we shouldn't make them feel bad or guilty about acknowledging it.

- **Suicide is taboo among today's teens:** Teens are beginning to embrace the topic of suicide more than adults in today's world. While parents and other adults are trying to figure out how to introduce the topic, teens have already researched it and understood it. Series like 13 Reasons Why (from Netflix) provides a realistic view of the topic of suicide. Sadly, some parents did not see the hype around the series as an opportunity to discuss the topic further with interested teens. One reason is that adults struggle with the topic of suicide themselves and would rather not broach the topic until it becomes an issue within their own family. But I think parents should take the opportunity to broach the topic when necessary.

- Most teens considering suicide want to live but don't know how: I truly appreciate and adore the beauty of life when it reveals how beautiful it can be. Nature and animals are beautiful, the land is mysteriously beautiful, relationships can be beautiful, freedom and education are fulfilling, etc. But when my lens changes from positive to negative due to the challenges of life, none of this matters at the time. People who are struggling with suicidal thoughts have this dilemma. On one side of the coin they want to live to experience the beauty of life, but on the other hand, they feel their freedom is just around the corner with one simple suicidal action. This roller-coaster keeps them confused. Experiencing more good days than bad days also keeps them in a state of limbo. This state of limbo causes them to want to live life at some times, while not wanting to live life at other times. Teens experience them too.

- **Some teens who think of suicide have no idea how to carry it out:** I previously had teen clients who would report thoughts of suicide (i.e., suicidal ideation) and intense feelings but had absolutely no plan. A plan would be the vehicle by which the suicide would be carried out (i.e., overdose, gun, knife, suicide by cop, etc). Some teens are even more afraid of suicide than homicide and may attempt to die by causing someone else to harm them. There are times I will inform parents that if there is no plan, the teen may attempt to provoke someone else to kill them such as a police officer (i.e., in the case of suicide by cop).

- **When a teen has suicidal thoughts, intent, and a plan we must carefully approach the issue:** Even if the individual has the thought, high intent, and a plan we must know how to handle the person in order to help them see the value of not acting. For example, when I meet with teens who are suicidal, have a high level of intent to complete the act, and has access to guns, pills, or weapons, I must take every opportunity I have to make our initial encounter positive, listen to the client, and help them see that there is still hope for a better outcome. When someone is at this stage, it is important to handle them carefully. We also should poke around for any apprehensive because this means there is still hope. In fact, of the 26 individuals who jumped from the Golden Gate Bridge, some report regretting it. Reports from www.newyorker.com state that of the 26 people who attempted to kill themselves on one of the most dangerous bridges in the nation, the ones who survived reported regretting that they jumped in the first place. One individual reported that the jump felt like an eternity on the way down. He reported wanting to change his decision the second his feet left the bridge. As I stated above, some individuals are conflicted about suicide and do not always want to die, even if they have thought(s). In cases where teens have severely harmed themselves in an attempt to die, they often walk away saying they will never do what they did again. Other teens, especially those with borderline personality traits, may up the ante. It is frightening to know that every 2 weeks, someone jumps off the Golden Gate Bridge in San Francisco. Can you believe that every second of the day someone, in the world, is considering suicide? When you put this fact into words and really start to explore how much of a problem suicide is, it's frightening. While we are distracted by our own lives, someone in the world is considering suicide. There isn't 1 second of the day where suicide is not thought of by at least 1 person. Someone somewhere is thinking about it. In fact, 4 out of 5 teens have given clear warning signs that they were considering suicide. No one saw it until it was too late. We must also keep in mind the influence of pop psychology, music, modern culture, and peers on teens who are considering suicide (we will discuss more of this in chapter 3 when we look at suicide-contagion). But when I have conversations about suicide with older teens (ages 15+), I recognize that many of their theories about the world around them are developed and reinforced by popular culture, primarily music and artistic literature. Believe it or not, artistic literature can be a very strong influence on youths who listen to multiple genres of music. One of my former teen clients and I discussed the Golden Gate Bridge and suicide after he shared a the lyrics of a hard-metal song with me. We learned that more than 3,000 people have jumped to their death from the Golden Gate Bridge. The $35 million dollar signature landmark bridge for San Francisco has assisted about 3,000 people in completing a suicide. It is designed by very strong wire and took multiple construction workers to build it. In fact, a plan was devised for the construction workers to have a "safety net" because in the construction of the dangerous bridge, about 11 construction workers died. Today, the community of San Francisco has also suggested a "suicide net" to help prevent the high number of suicides the state has. As you can see, the bridge is quite dangerous and has been called the infamous spot for people contemplating suicide. The very fact that 3,000 + people considered suicide and completed it should shake you at your core. It did for me and my teen client. It is frightening to think that so many people would want to die and that one bridge could assist so many in their deaths. The day my teen client and I evaluated this reality was the day he informed me that many of his suicidal thoughts were reinforced by the music and literature he was reading. He really taught me a valuable fact that affects millions of teens today. As you will see in chapter 5, suicide-contagion is brought to life because of the influence others have on each other.

- **Most teens think of suicide but shy away from mentioning it:** Would you share your suicidal thoughts with someone you believe would never understand, who would never react empathically to you, or who would undermine or minimize your pain? Why would you? I wouldn't and I'm sure you wouldn't either. As a result, many teens considering suicide quietly "send" signals, gather the tools to complete their plan, and then go forward with it.

- **Philosophy freely discussed suicide and viewed it as a dilemma of being human and so do teens:** Philosophers such as Kant, Plato, Friedrich Nietzsche, or Socrates all discussed suicide including many other philosophers. In fact, Plato discussed that suicide was disgraceful and that these people should be buried without tombs or markings to identify them. Does this sound like a similar attitude held by many people in today's society? Of course. This is why so many people shy away from mentioning suicide. It stigmatizes. Sadly, Plato saw suicide as a cowardly act. Kant viewed suicide as irrational and felt that self-preservation was important to the universe. Philosophers have long battled in the debate of suicide. Sadly, some people hold very rigid views of suicide that imprison's many suffering people.

- **There is often conflicting thoughts and feelings about suicide within the teen considering it:** Dr. Lisa Firestone, from the Glendon Association, studies suicide and violence. She reported that for many of the individuals who survived the jump from the Golden Gate Bridge displayed ambivalence which is always a factor in suicide. For me, I have seen many of my teen clients struggle with conflicting thoughts and emotions.

- **Suicidal tendencies are being influenced by genes, environment, and trauma:** Research suggests that suicidal tendencies tend to occur in families where trauma has occurred, where individuals are predisposed to certain mental health conditions such as depression, and in an un-nurturing, invalidating, or a complicated family environment.

- **Negative self-talk, rumination, thinking errors, and an internal locus of control all can lead to suicidal

thoughts: Individuals who struggle with negative thoughts and self-talk, rumination (thinking of an event repeatedly and feeling depressed or anxious about the thought), and internal locus of control (i.e., believing that values, thoughts, or other personal characteristics are to blame for challenges in one's life) can struggle with depression which can lead to suicidal thoughts. It is a dangerous cycle.

Putting it all together

Identifying teens who are suicidal can seem like one of the most difficult things you will ever have to do. Teens are smart. They may not be fully mature or ready to broach the topics we think they should be ready to broach. But that doesn't mean they aren't thinking about life, seeing life as difficult, or desiring a less complicated life. Some teens are very "deep" and spiritually awakened. Others are logical and smart. And still others may be so immature that they haven't even thought about life long enough to feel suicidal. Wherever your teen is on this spectrum, just let them know (the best way you can) that you are there for them when/if they are ready to talk. I know you must love your teen or you would not be reading this book. But sometimes, as a therapist, I feel the need to remind parents to just love their teens. Loving your teen doesn't mean always calling them out on their behaviors, thoughts, or feelings. It doesn't always mean giving them everything they ask for or giving them "freedom." Sometimes it just means being present, being aware, and being a barrier between their suicidal thoughts and themselves. As you continue reading this book, I hope that you feel increasingly more empowered to be a smart parent with a strategic plan to help your teen prevent their own suicide.

Answers to thinking errors activity

Thinking error # 1: Generalization and black/white thinking

Thinking error # 2: Existential thinking, questioning of faith

Thinking error #3: Generalization, negative self-talk, and nihilistic thinking

Thinking error #4: Negative self-talk and delusional beliefs

NOTES

Chapter 3

Developing A Clear Understanding of Teen Suicide-contagion

"I didn't want to wake up. I was having a much better time asleep. And that's really sad. It was almost like a reverse nightmare, like when you wake up from a nightmare you're so relieved. I woke up into a nightmare."

—**Ned Vizzini, It's Kind of a Funny Story**

Globally, suicide is the 2nd leading cause of death among individuals ages 15 to 29 years old. According to the World Health Organization (WHO), 800,000 people die by suicide around the world every single year. That's similar to about 1 person committing suicide every 4o seconds. Can you imagine? Can you imagine the emotional and psychological pain of those 800,000 people who die every year? I wouldn't blame you if you found it difficult to understand. I've often wondered if those 800,000 people all died for the same reasons. Could there be some psychological phenomenon at play in the lives of these individuals? Or are they individuals who all simply want to die?

One of the difficult parts of writing a book about suicide is the fact that sharing certain details or information has the potential of resulting in more suicides. Have you ever heard of the term *suicide contagion*? Suicide contagion is a concept that describes an individual who observes another individual who has committed suicide and therefore begins to think seriously about taking his or her own life. The term is often referred to as "The Werther Effect" (i.e., the phenomenon of copycat suicides). The term was created after the novel *Die Leiden des jungen Werthers* (The Sorrows of Youth Werther) written by Goethe in 1774. After the book's publication, men from various walks of life began to mimic the dress style of the men in the novel and then would kill themselves. The association between the book's publication and the suicides sparked interest and fear which led to the term "The Werther Effect." The Werther Effect or copycat suicides of the time resulted in the book being banned. The term "suicide contagion" was later coined, in 1974, by researcher David Phillips to describe the act of people within society committing suicide because of a highly publicized or "attention-grabbing" suicide. Glorification of suicide continues to studied in today's literature, publicized on social media and reported in research studies. This too can lead to an increase of suicides. In fact, after the airing of the popular teen series from Netflix *13 Reasons Why* the term "Suicide Contagion" returned to the scene. A study published in the peer-reviewed medical journal, the JAMA Internal Medicine, found the series was associated with an increase in Internet searches of suicide, including a 26% increase in searches for "how to commit suicide," an 18% increase for "commit suicide" and a 9% increase for "how to kill yourself." The sad part about all of this is that most of society is uninformed about this pattern of behavior which means that teens are able to slip through the cracks because adults aren't watching.

Many research studies over the years have been conducted on the contagiousness of suicide within pockets of our society such as among teenage groups, religious sects or pacts, and other groups that share a some kind of similar mission. It is very likely that your teen would follow the behavior of a deceased adolescent who may have received a lot of attention and praise after his or her death. I firmly believe that open communication, building awareness, and allowing teens to discuss their thoughts and feelings may reduce this possibility.

In some cases the behavior of one teen can strongly influence the behavior of other teens in the same environment. A trauma-related concept known as *collective disturbance* may help you understand this phenomenon a bit better.

"Red Flag" meetings and collective disturbance

I observed suicide contagion while working in a residential treatment facility (RTF) for at-risk youths, youths adjudicated delinquent, and youths with psychotic symptoms. One adolescent attempted suicide by hanging herself in the bathroom with her bathrobe tie. She almost succeeded but thankfully staff heard a noise and responded immediately. She was pale, had blue lips, and was very close to dying. The other residents between the ages of 13 and 17 years old observed the entire incident. A couple days later, other adolescents within the program began attempting suicide. This led to what we call a red flag meeting. As mentioned at the beginning of the book, The Sanctuary Model of Trauma-Informed Care includes red flag meetings. *Red flag meetings* are scheduled during times when very important conversations need to be discussed. The meeting is lead by the person who called the meeting and the goal of the meeting is to come to a consensus on how a difficult situation can be successfully resolved. The Sanctuary Model includes a manual for staff as well as training so they may understand how to lead these meetings successfully. I think "red flag meetings" can also happen at home and in the school setting. In fact, parent-teacher conferences and "family meetings" have many of the same elements of a red flag meeting. However, the difference with the red flag meeting is that the following is emphasized:

- The meeting begins with what is called community meeting. This includes focusing on certain elements specific to that person for the day. For example, an individual who is apart of the meeting may report their goal for participating, their idea of what a resolution would be, and how they are feeling.
- The person who called for the red flag meeting would explain why they feel the meeting is needed at the time.
- The participants will describe what happened, what triggered it, what isn't working, etc.
- A plan for resolution of the problem is discussed.
- Another meeting is scheduled so everyone may discuss what is or is not working. Everyone agrees

to contribute to the environment in positive ways.

Red flag meetings always have at the foundation of its principles an awareness of trauma or an awareness of the things that makes each individual vulnerable to continual problems. For example, if you decide to have a "red flag" meeting with your family, you will want to keep in mind the vulnerabilities or risk factors that may make your family or teen vulnerable to further difficulties. If your teenager is attempting suicide for the 3rd time and you feel you need to have a "red flag" meeting with your teen, you should keep in mind that emotional pressure, stress, confrontation, and embarrassment may be a trigger that can make things a whole lot worse. You want to ensure that some kind of resolution is achieved such as going to therapy more times during the week, your teen promising to call you every 2-3 hours when away from home, or you and your teen agreeing to have discussions every month of their emotional well-being. Red flag meetings are also held at times when the youths in the environment are calm enough to handle difficult conversations. You wouldn't want to have a conversation with your teen when he or she is extremely stressed with school, a breakup, or bullying. Choose your time to have significant conversations wisely. The goal isn't the meeting itself, but rather the collective decision-making that can lead to better behaviors and communication.

Sadly, when teens are admitted to RTF programs, some of the staff aren't trained well enough to execute these meetings appropriately which can sometimes result in more problems among the residents. In my situation the youths admitted to the RTF began to challenge staff, hide sharp objects in their bedroom, refuse to see the psychiatrist when called, lie about swallowing medication, and idolize suicide. In group homes or RTF's suicide Contagion can be one of the most difficult hits to the environment, often results in in what is known as *collective disturbance.* Collective disturbance is a state of disequilibrium in which everyone in the environment is caught off-guard and remains off for long periods of time. A cascade of incidents may occur and everyone may end up reacting to each other in inappropriate ways. An example of this would be in the case of a family who has a father with a severe alcohol addiction and challenges with anger management. The father may get drunk, begin to physically assault his wife which results in the teenage children getting involved, and then everyone in the house fighting each other. The police may arrive to calm things but everyone involved (including the police) beings to react out of emotion and anger. Things can escalate to the point of the police having to use physical force to calm and apprehend the father. The father and the teen children go to jail for assault and the mother is left with nothing but memories of a tragic situation. In this example, no one wins because everyone including the police acted out of emotion. This is collective disturbance.

I would not doubt that collective disturbance is at the core of suicide contagion within school environments. It's as if everyone in the environment begins to "catch suicide" as a disease and therefore begins to believe that suicide is the answer. Sometimes the suicide contagion influences teens to kill themselves because they feel indebted to another teen who killed themselves. This mindset is often found in situations where adolescents bond and feel connected through similar struggles in life, challenges in school, beliefs, religious affiliation, and/or some other spiritual or psychological cause. This is why it is very important that teachers (and schools) understand suicide among teenagers so they can be ready to respond to those teens who are struggling.

A brief historical and modern view of suicide-contagion

According to the Centre for Suicide Prevention, suicide is the leading cause of death for ingenous youth in Canada. It is an epidemic. In a note left behind in February of 2017 by Jenara Roundsky, one of the 12 year old girls living in the remote Wapekeka First Nation community in Northwestern Canada, she stated "suicide people are just angels wanting to go home." Sadly, reports indicate that this young lady fell through the cracks of the system. In an interview from CBS News, Roundsky's uncle, Joshua Frogg, reported "there was no plan of care, there was no safety plan for her." Roundsky had been on suicide watch.

Suicide contagion is an old term used to describe a perpetual condition that needs further study. Suicide-contagion was a tragedy that struck Wapekeka First Nation, an indigenous community of about 400 people. On January 8, 2017 Jolynn Winters took her own life after making a suicide pact with two other 12 year old girls she befriended. Not only did these deaths rock the foundation of all the residents in the small community, but it also pulled the covers off of Chantel Fox, one of the youths who made a pact to end her life as well. Reports indicate that Jenara was the first to take her life, and that Chantel Fox took her life 2 days after Jolynn committed suicide as well. A few days after Fox's death, four other youths were flown out of the community for intervention and medical treatment. The suicides prompted a call for an emergency response team. Despite leaders declaring a state of emergency asking for suicide prevention resources and greater protections for at risk youth, the deaths haunted the residents for months. Suicide-contagion within isolated and rual communities pack a powerful punch.

    Many of the residents of the indigenous community reported asking for help from the Canadian government for suicide prevention resources after they learned of Winters and Fox. Community news reports indicate that the request took some time to be acknowledged and when it was, it was "too late." The government reported that they wanted to assist the community and provide funds for better resources but the request came at a time when the funds were already allocated. The community remains in need of suicide prevention resources today. If it wasn't bad enough that the only way for "outsiders" to enter the community was through airplane, 10% of the community remained at risk for more suicides following the deaths of the Jenara and Jolynn. And this isn't the only case that reveals the need for greater awareness of suicide-contagion.

It's amazing to see just how the instigating suicide serves as a type of "model" to others in the same environment. Not one of the observers of the suicides had the strength or psychological capacity to refuse to follow. Instead, each individual above followed the other. I'm sure reading this, as a parent, makes you even more afraid of suicide than you were to begin with. I don't blame you. It is a topic that can shake you at your core and hold you hostage in fear. Many parents who discuss these events with me during sessions almost always display a look of shock, confusion, and horror on their faces as I describe the events in some detail for psychoeducation on suicide-contagion. I've seen a common thread which is that parents can't seem to fathom how to share this topic with their teen for fear of putting the thought in their minds. But then I ask the following question: "How would you feel if your 8th grade pre-teen had a slumber party that resulted in two suicides?" Probably the same exact way parents of Haylee Fentress and Paige Moravetz felt after finding out their teens had made a suicide pact to kill themselves during a sleepover. Multiple news reports suggest that bullying was at the heart of the suicide pact. The Minnesota teens reportedly felt bullied by fellow 8th graders in their school which led the girls to consider a way out. Fentress and Moravetz wrote a suicide note and then hanged themselves. They were both found by Fentress's mother, while Moravetz's parents were on vacation in Hawaii.

The question begs to be answered "what could have prevented this?" The answer isn't as easy as we would like it to be. But I firmly believe that open communication and adult awareness of teen emotional challenges could stop a lot of teen suicides.

Social media and the influence of suicide-contagion

When I see parents and their teens for family therapy after an attempted suicide, I broach the topic of religious cults, teen "support groups," online teen chat-rooms, and other places where teens gather to discuss popular culture, art, music, and their emotional and psychological states. This is often a very important conversation I have with parents because many parents lack knowledge and information about the powerful influence teen groups have on each other. Many of these groups are online in today's society. This means that you, as a parent of a modern-day youth, must learn the lingo and the popular ways teens communicate these days. Social media chat sites such as GroupMe, Kik Messenger, WhatsApp, and Musical.ly should be researched or at least Google searched. I'm sure you have heard of (and maybe even used) sites such as Twitter, Myspace, Instagram, Facebook, Snapchat, and Tubler. But you'll want to do research on the less popular apps as many of today's teens are moving on to sneakier ways of communicating. You'll also want to know more about video chats and streaming such as Houseparty, Live.ly, Live.me, YouNow, Monkey, and Whisper. And don't forget about the popular app Snapchat. Teens love this tool because it allows them to put a "time limit," so they think, on their posts or shares. But sadly, content is data and data online never truly goes away, according to Commonsensemedia.org. I've heard of teens taking pictures of the so-called instant posts and photos in order to keep them. Data online is easy to hack and really smart hackers can probably locate the information (as in the major hack of SnapChat in December of 2013 that involved a settlement with the FTC). I'm sure you will get some push back from your teen if you broach this topic. Don't be afraid of that. Your teen needs to know that these are very important issues and that you will not permit them to stay in the dark, despite what their friends are saying and doing. Someone has to be enlightened and it should be your teen. It may also be a good idea to share this information with your teen's school, primarily, his or her teacher. Teachers can funnel this information to others in the school and maybe even have a class dedicated to teaching students about the dangers of these apps.

Religious cults and the influence of suicide-contagion

Although the following devastating case did not involve teens, it is still important to discuss as many teens are highly influenced by groups with strong opinions. In 1974 a religious sect group was formed by Marshall Applewhite and Bonnie Nettles. Heaven's Gate was a religious cult based out of San Diego, California and included about 39 members. The group's "mission" was to identify UFO's and engage in extreme self-reunification which resulted in castration. The group existed under a variety of names over the years as if it wanted to hide and escape ever being truly found out. The only notariety the group received was after the 39 members committed suicide in a suburban area of San Diego in March of 1997. News reports and studies that include the history of this group report that both Applewhite and Nettles believed they were the witnesses mentioned in the book of Revelations (Revelations chapter 11) in the Bible. The story goes that when their hope of leaving the earth for a "higher level" existence did not come while living in a remote area of Texas, Applewhite and Nettles moved to California to wait on a "higher level" of living with the few followers they attracted. It appears the cult began many rounds of proselytization (i.e. to induce someone to convert to one's religious beliefs). Sadly, many of the "devout" followers did not understand the full extent of their unstable beliefs and that they were ultimately divested of their rights by Applewhite and Nettles. The women including their small amount of followers created a website in which they communicated with some of the outside world. After their group diminished to only 39 members (most likely because of the ridiculousness of their cause), rumors circulated that a UFO or spaceship would be coming close to earth. As the Comet Hale-Bopp approached the earth, "Heaven's Gate" members drank poison in 3 waves of 15, 15, and 9 strongly believing the delusion that the spaceship would come close enough to earth to "rescue" them and take them to a better place, hence the name "Heaven's Gate." Stories of the incident reveal that the members created a video explaining their reasons for believing as they did. Suicide-contagion in this case seems more like a suicide-cluster. A suicide-cluster is a group of suicides (often involving people with similar objects, events, or other elements) in which one suicide seems to set off the other. In other words, suicide-clusters involve a cascade or chain of completed suicides. Simply put, it is copycat suicide.

Putting it all together

So what do we do about such incidents and can we prevent them? That question is difficult to answer and will require further attention, study, education, research, and money to fund prevention programs (especially in indigenous, remote, and rural communities). It is not enough to just talk about these incidents and bring awareness. We need to put into action efforts aimed at reducing these suicides. The commonality in each incident discussed above is suicide-contagion. In order to reduce the amount of suicides that occur each year because of copycats or individuals highly influenced by suicide-clusters we must discuss the powerful influence of these events on the hearts and minds of those left behind.

The echos of the voices of the young pre-teens who took their lives will reverberate forever in the conscience of their parents. Could they have done something to stop this? Why didn't they see this coming? I'm sure their parents had these and many more questions long after the suicides. I hope these questions, your voice, and my support of you will encourage you to step out and speak on these issues. Even more, I hope you will talk to your teen about these incidents and educate them to the emotional and psychological toll they take on the nation as a whole.

NOTES

CHAPTER 4

What To Do And Where To Start

"The way we talk to our children becomes their inner voice."

- Peggy O' Mara

Did you know that suicide is most prevalent among youths between the ages of 15 and 24? Research on neuroscience suggests that the human brain is not fully developed, primarily the frontal lobes (an area behind the forehead responsible for executive functioning such as decision-making, impulse control, and personality development) until around the age of 25 years old. Until this age, youngsters may find it difficult to balance their feelings, thoughts, and behaviors and control their impulses. Without the ability to control thinking and negative feelings that lead to risky behaviors, it may be difficult for them to examine their situation, weigh the pros and cons of their decision(s), and ultimately choose the most appropriate path. That's why with many of my own clients I encourage parents to be involved in at least every other session if they are not seeing me weekly for family sessions. Parents can often be great role-models of self-control.

Parents, teachers, and other responsible adults in the lives of young people have such a powerful impact on their decision-making. While some teenagers may bulk at the advice or suggestion of an adult, most teens do accept suggestions or advice of those they respect. For example, I once had a 13-year-old male client who refused to listen to anything his parents or I would say. He was headed down the wrong road by hanging out with other adolescents who had a negative self-image and reputation in the school for using drugs and alcohol on school grounds. On one occasion he was caught using drugs in the boy's bathroom which resulted in detention, meetings with the Principal, and suggestions for counseling in a hospitalization or residential setting. His parents and I would have long conversations about the consequences of befriending negative peers and allowing them to influence his decisions and behaviors. Despite tedious sessions that included his parents lecturing him and begging him to change, he maintained his friendship with these peers. As a result, he became suicidal and homicidal on multiple occasions. However, once in college and facing the same situation from high school, he decided that his future was more important than "hanging out" with college guys who only wanted to party and date. He discussed this with me during one of his "maintenance" sessions (i.e., a session that occurs 1-2x per month as a way to follow-up and discuss potential concerns).

He explained:

> "even though you and my parents think I wasn't listening all those times you lectured me, I was. I needed help. I was suicidal, depressed, and didn't know who I was. I tried so hard to ignore what you and my parents said. But I realize that you and my parents were right. I couldn't control my behavior and I didn't know how to say "no" to them. I wanted friends but never got what I wanted. So, I became suicidal and even more depressed. As a man now I really despise my actions. I don't want to be this way. Now that I'm in college, I need to make better decisions. But I still have suicidal thoughts and my parents can't understand why. But I remember everything you and my parents told me."

I once had a mother ask me why her daughter would ever consider suicide. I remember explaining to her that suicidal thoughts are sometimes the only way a teenager can imagine a way out of their pain. For all humans, we look for ways to increase pleasure or happy experiences and decrease pain and suffering. While one individual may drink and use drugs to cope, others may think of ways to end all of their pain through suicide. For some teens, using drugs, engaging in risky behaviors, having multiple and risky sexual experiences, gambling, overspending, etc. may be the best way for them to "erase" their pain. But for other youths, it is suicide. These behaviors are often ways teens may try to cope with life when it gets painful. Suicidal thoughts are no different. In some ways, suicidal thoughts serve as a coping skill for some teens, despite this coping skill being a negative one.

Identifying the problem for the first time

When I meet with parents who have concerns that their teenager may be considering suicide I offer psycho-education (i.e., education about the topic of suicide in a therapeutic fashion) and strive to make parents, like you, feel empowered enough to spot signs in your teen. Some of the signs that an adolescent may be considering suicide include but are not limited to:

- **Using "passive-death wish" statements:** Passive-death wishes are statements that an individual may make to "test the waters" and to see what others may say in response to the statement. For example, a person may say, "I wonder what it would be like to die" or "I wonder how everyone would feel if I weren't around anymore." Sometimes these statements are made out of anger or vindictiveness but at other times, they are used to "survey" other people. "Surveying" other people is a nice way to gain information or determine the reaction of others by making an indirect statement. Teenagers often use passive-death wishes when speaking with adults about how they feel about their life. It is important to be able to spot them. They come in many shapes and many forms. I have listed a variety of ways teenagers may use passive-death wishes to communicate their feelings in Appendix A. It may be useful to share these passive-death wish statements with your teen's teacher so that they will also understand what these statements sound like. You can also make a list of statements your teen has made and share with your teen's teacher. You would want to consider the age of your teen, their personality style, and the relationship they have with their teacher. You wouldn't want to share a quiet 15 year old's statements with a very direct and distant teacher. This may "scare" the teen away from sharing any more of their thoughts and feelings.

- **Having a suicide plan with a high level of intent:** Mature and smart teenagers may have thought out suicide so much that they have created a detailed plan on how they would carry out their wishes and when. Teenagers who have a suicide plan and a high level of intent to carry out that plan would be considered lethal and to be in imminent danger. As a result, hospitalization needs to occur as soon as possible. In order for a teen to be admitted to the hospital for psychiatric care, he or she must have a clear plan to commit suicide (i.e., cutting the wrist, using a weapon such as a gun, overdosing, etc.) and a high level of intent (i.e., a high level of motivation to complete the act). In some cases, a teen may be sent home (sometimes due to limited bed availability) if they are able to keep themselves safe and has little to no access to "tools" to carry out a suicide. For example, in one of my previous cases I had a 12-year-old client who had written a thorough suicide plan, had a high level of intent to commit suicide, and told me "I'm just waiting for the right moment." The hospital released her 5 hours after a clinical evaluation and reported to me that due to the client being in a residential facility with 24/7 supervision with little to no access to lethal means, she was being sent home. The hospital did not see admission as necessary at that time. Even more, for many youngsters hospitals act as "holding places" for those who are lethal or highly motivated to kill themselves. Hospitals are not safe havens that cradle the individual until they are absolutely stable. Most hospitals keep individuals for 24-72hrs and discharge them with a plan for further care. In many cases, those who have a high level of intent to kill themselves may end up back in the hospital days, if not hours, later.

- **Having a history of impulsivity and poor decision-making:** Individuals who are impulsive or inpatient and have a history of making poor decisions, may be considered lethal. What I mean by this is that these teens are most likely able to complete the act of suicide because of impulsivity, impatience, or an inability to consider the consequences of this final act. With limited executive functioning and brain maturity, teens are likely to seek instant gratification and for many suicidal teens, instant gratification may be death. These youngsters would benefit from a thorough crisis support plan and safety plan (see Appendix B for safety plan). If you are concerned that your teen may be struggling with suicidal thoughts, it is important to consider the impact of any clinical diagnoses they may have. Teens who struggle with a long history of Attention Deficit Hyperactivity Disorder, Borderline Personality Disorder, Psychosis (delusions or hallucinations), or high levels of anxiety are sometimes the most lethal. These youngsters will require more supervision, more support, and more guidance.

- **Having a history of vindictive or emotionally unstable responses to stress:** I once had a colleague who counseled a young female client with borderline personality traits and a history of oppositional defiant disorder say multiple times that she wanted to kill herself because her boyfriend broke up with her. She would call him and leave random messages on his voicemail every single day. Although he refused to respond and made his decision final not to respond to her, she continued to call him with threats of taking her life. He would then respond but later feel manipulated as her "suicidal thoughts" would mysteriously subside after speaking with him. This back-and-forth game continued until he recognized a pattern of vindictiveness and manipulation. Sadly, after she dropped out of therapy when her therapist pointed out this manipulation, no further contact could be made as she moved and changed her phone number. Adolescents who struggle with emotional instability, poor decision-making, and impulsivity may struggle the most with suicidal thoughts.

- **Writing or keeping a suicide note:** A suicide note is often the ONLY proof you need that your teen has strongly considered suicide. If you find a note, it is important to consider whether you should address the teen directly, encourage the teen to pursue and accept therapy, or contact a crisis support immediately. A suicide note is often a strong predictor of completed suicides including a history of suicide attempts. It is my personal belief and experience that suicide notes are written out of frustration, pain, or another strong emotion. It can be the only way a teen can get across that they are hurting. Adolescents may also secretly wish that an adult would see the letter and approach them about it to either initiate treatment, offer emotional support and attention, or help them figure out what to do.

Approaching a teen who has written a suicide note can be very challenging. Some adolescents become defensive and angry, while others may feel relieved that their note has been found. It has been my experience that most teens write suicide notes as a way of making their death "less painful" or "shocking" to the person who may find the note. Other teens may write the note as a cry for help. I previously worked with a 13-year-old student who was contemplating suicide and reporting suicidal thoughts to her teacher daily. The teacher reported that her thoughts were not only gruely, but psychotic. Although her teacher attempted multiple times to encourage her parents to pursue mental health treatment after finding suicide notes on her desk at school, her parents failed to make the appointments. The student later admitted that she wanted someone to find the notes. After months of writing suicide notes in hopes of being found out, she wrote her final suicide note, went to school as if nothing was wrong, and premeditated how she would kill herself while her parents were out of town on a business trip. The day she wrote the suicide note was the day she killed herself in the family's closed garage while running her father's car. The suicide note was taped to the inside of the garage door with multiple apologies for having hurt everyone.

It is extremely important that you take suicide notes seriously, while also being careful not to panic. Panicking will only result in your teen resisting you. Your calm demeanor is sometimes the only hope the teen has for help.

How parents can approach the topic of suicide with a teen

There are a few ways adults can approach a teen who has written a suicide note without triggering their defenses and anger. Some of the ways include:

- Asking about the note in a calm and nonchalant fashion. Teens will often resist a parent who addresses the teen in an angry rage, with a judgmental tone of voice, or shock. Most teens appreciate a calm and mature response to something they have done. Because there may be a lot of shame connected to the suicide note, it is important that parents set aside a good time to discuss the note with the teen and calmly facilitate discussion.

- Avoid judging and minimizing. Many of the teenagers I currently work with prefer to share their emotions, thoughts, and challenges with adults who are able to listen to them, relate to their feelings, understand why they did what they did, and simply listen. When an adult begins to judge, criticize, question in a condescending tone of voice, or strongly oppose them, the teen automatically shuts down and in order to protect their fragile sense of self, they stop talking. Your job as a parent who has found a suicide note is not to chastise, judge, or criticize. Your job is to gather some facts on why your teen has chosen this route. If your teen maintains a defensive demeanor and refuses to open up, you'll want to explain what the next steps are that you are likely to take such as talking with your family doctor (who can make mental health referrals), pursuing treatment, and possibly even medication.

- Inform the teen's teacher by email first, then in person, if needed. You will want to inform your teen's teacher(s) about some of the challenges they are having. You don't have to allude specifically to suicidal thoughts but you could make it known that your child is struggling with difficult emotions and may not be themselves. You can also include that you are pursuing treatment and would appreciate if the teacher(s) could email you with any concerns. If you prefer to steer clear of teachers, you can relay this same information to the school psychologist or guidance counselor. It is important that schools know what is going on so that when or if they find out what is happening, they will understand that you are working on supporting your teen (see the end of this chapter for a sample letter to the school).

Involving the school

As a parent, you may feel absolutely vulnerable during the entire process of learning of your teen's suicidal thoughts. Because of this, shame, guilt, anger, and confusion may prevent you from reaching out to the teen's school for support. But you must remember that reaching out means possibly getting services within the school to assist your struggling teen. Some services include but are not limited to: an Individualized Education Plan (IEP) for emotional and learning support, a 504 plan (a plan that permits teens to have accommodations for completing schoolwork), or a tutor. The school counselor or school psychologist can also "keep an eye out" for teens who have a history of suicidal thoughts or attempts. Involving the school also means maintaining open communication necessary for keeping the teen safe and stable. As a parent, you control how much information you want the school to know. You don't have to divulge everything. You can provide only the facts and ask that the school counselor or psychologist support your teen as needed. You can also have the teen's school sign a consent to speak with the therapist or treatment provider working with you. Doing so will ensure that everyone is on the same page and is able to coordinate treatment so that everyone can come up with a plan on how to best support your teen.

If for any reason you decide the school does not need to know about every suicidal thought or behavior your teen shares with you, I encourage you to inform at least 1-2 other teachers and other professionals working with your teen. This ensures that your teen will be monitored. A primarily care physician or family doctor, mental health therapist or psychologist, or psychiatrist should know about everything that is happening with a suicidal adolescent. This ensures that the teen's treatment team is able to make adjustments to medication, alter therapeutic approaches, or best meet the teen's needs. You should also keep in mind that if you sign a consent for a teacher or school to speak with your teen's treatment provider(s), you can always withdraw that consent. Providers or schools who have consent to be engaged in a teen's treatment are legally bound to respect your request to withdraw consent.

Helping teens regain stability and a balanced view

Sometimes it feels like the hardest job in the world to motivate teens to do what is in their best interest. With the advent of pseudo-maturity, feelings of independence, and more freedom, it can sometimes feel like an impossible task to get an adolescent to acknowledge their need for support, accept the need for counseling, and engage in therapeutic activities. For many of the adolescent clients I work with, the only reason they are in therapy is because the parent or the teen's school is requiring them to engage in therapy. As a result, parents (and sometimes teachers) end up feeling as if their best efforts to support the teen is being ignored and unappreciated. The teen, however, may not fully understand these feelings because all they see are their own feelings and challenges. They may also feel that they are being punished for hiding or expressing their suicidal thoughts. These feelings can result in resentment and lack of trust from all individuals involved. As a result, it is not uncommon for a parent or teacher to connect with the teen's therapist and express concerns that the teen is not taking treatment seriously and is continuing to avoid accountability.

It will be very important that therapists, parents, and teachers make it clear to the teen that they are not being punished, even though it may feel that way. They should understand that treatment is being pursued because everyone involved cares. Parents and teachers should continue working with the teen's therapist on helping them see the usefulness of therapy. This may take time and that is okay. If it takes too much time, however, parents or teachers should address the teen and ask them what is preventing them from benefiting. If the answer is complicated, it may be useful to speak to the teen's therapist about this "bump in the road" and ways to overcome it.

Sometimes the way to overcome "bumps in the road" include but are not limited to:

Medication management: Adolescents who are struggling with suicidal thoughts are often also struggling with depression, anxiety, or symptoms of another mental health diagnosis. Because of this, medication management may be useful in helping the teen regain internal stability (i.e., the stability of their thoughts, feelings, and behaviors). Medication is not the it-all, but rather crutch to help teens re-focus, gain some internal control, and possibly put more effort into therapy. Medication can make the process of therapy a bit easier for some teens. Also, keep in mind that medication doesn't have to mean a lifelong use of it. It might just mean a few months or a year of medication therapy until the teen is able to feel stable again.

More or less therapy: Some adolescents are not ready to be thrown into therapy, especially if it is for the first time. Many of my adolescent clients reported their first experiences in therapy to be "intrusive," "weird," and "uncomfortable." Therapy can certainly feel intrusive to adults much less teenagers. Week after week you sit across from a person who is observing you for an entire hour, making statements to cause you to think deeper about things, and who has certain opinions, thoughts, and feelings about you. For teens, this feels like punishment. For these youngsters, less therapy may be helpful. Seeing a therapist 1 time per week for 2 months, 1 time a week for a month, 2 times a week for 1 month, etc. may be helpful until they get the hang of therapy. Introducing the idea of therapy one step at a time may coerce resistant teen. As the teen begins to develop rapport and trust with the therapist, therapy will be easier.

It can be comforting to some teens if they understand the process of therapy, the length of therapy, and the goal. In my experience I have observed that if I explain everything to the teenager during the first and second sessions, it positively changed the teen's behavior, the parent, and sometimes even the teacher(s) involved. As the adolescent becomes more comfortable with treatment and open to learning and growing, the parent(s) and/or teacher(s) can take a few steps back and permit the teen to make some decisions and grow on their own. It is a freeing experience.

For other teens, more therapy may be helpful in kick-starting "recovery." Some teens would benefit from intensive services (as you will see in chapter 5). Teens who are not responding well in therapy may need to therapy more times throughout the week in order to truly benefit from concepts discussed, tools provided, and techniques learned. For suicidal adolescents that come to me for therapy, I tend to see them at least 2x per week and once stabilized, I reduce the number of sessions to 1x per week and then 1 time biweekly. I have seen suicidal teens up to 3 times per week to stabilize them. We then would reduce sessions to 2 times a week and then 1 time a week.

The right therapist: Most adults would agree that if there is no emotional or social connection between two people a relationship of any kind is not going to work. Why would a teenager be any different? An adolescent has to be able to connect with someone before they are able to fully in treatment services. The right therapist may be difficult to find and may take time. The time spent pursuing the right therapist can be time-consuming and emotionally draining but ultimately worth the effort. If a teen does not feel comfortable with someone who is asking them questions, engaging them in conversation, and observing them, they are not going to open up or fully engage in therapy. Why would they? Finding the right therapist is very important for teens, especially those who are resistant to treatment.

Reacting with empathy

It can be very difficult for parents and teachers to find out that an adolescent is contemplating suicide. Your teen's confession of suicidal thoughts may trigger very strong emotions in you which can come off to your teen as insensitive or angry. Teens who feel the adult views them negatively will most likely continue to suffer in silence. As a result, we must learn to respond with empathy (i.e., compassion, understanding, and care) and control immediate reactions. Facial expressions, tone of voice, body language, and attitude are important to control so that the teen will open up and feel accepted and loved enough to share their deepest feelings. Would you share your feelings with someone who seemed disappointed in you, angry, or insensitive? Although your reactions may be the result of the love and care you feel for your teen, your teen is likely to misperceive your reaction(s). As you know, adolescents can be very difficult to read and many of them struggle with balanced perception of reality. Their emotions are often all over the place and their needs and wants tend to mesh. So the involvement of empathic parent(s) and teacher(s) will be essential at this time.

Case study of Stephanie

Let's meet Stephanie and her parents, Kimberly and Steve. Stephanie was a 15-year-old student that I worked with when I provided individual, family, and group therapy in a school-based program designed to rehabilitate and educate juvenile delinquents. She struggled with emotion dysregulation since the age of 5. Her emotional outbursts were so bad that her parents had to lock themselves in their bedroom until she calmed down. Stephanie was born 4 weeks premature, remained in the hospital for 3 weeks after birth due to health concerns, and once home, struggled with colic. By kindergarten, Stephanie had developed mood swings, oppositional behavior, and a lot of attitude. By the time she got to 10th grade she had become extremely unruly to the point of her parents having to call the police on her for fear of their own safety. I met with Stephanie for the first time following a series of arrests connected to drug charges.

My first meeting with Stephanie alone

Me: Hi Stephanie. My name is Tàmara and I will be your therapist while you are serving probation. How are you?

Stephanie: Hi.

Me: Could you tell me a bit about why you are here? It appears you are a good kid.

Stephanie: Well...I'm not all that good.

Me: How come?

Stephanie: Well...I would think you would have this information already, but I'll tell you anyway. I got mad at my parents because they told me I could date this boy and then later changed their mind because they found out he was selling drugs while I was at his house.

Me: Wow. What was your response to that?

Stephanie: I was mad! HOW CAN YOU TELL ME I COULD DATE SOMEONE AND THEN LATER CHANGE YOUR MIND?! They don't know me. I get mad real fast.

Me: I see. I don't really blame you. When your parent tells you that you can date someone that gives you the go-ahead to fall for that person even more and "invite" them into your life. Do you know what I mean?

Stephanie: Yeah. That makes sense. Then I got real mad and smashed my dad's car windows.

Me: I think you were more hurt than angry because you most likely had your hopes up for something positive with this guy. Am I close?

Stephanie: Yeah, that's right. I did. I would think of him all of the time in school, after school, at night, and when I would get up. I guess I loved him.

Me: Perhaps. Or perhaps you needed him for some kind of emotional support you felt you didn't have elsewhere in your life.

Stephanie: Yeah. Maybe. I was so hurt that I thought of killing myself.

Me: Oh God. What happened?

Stephanie: The night my parents and I started to argue about it I stormed upstairs and looked at a bottle of pills my boyfriend was going to sell for money. I picked them up, counted how many there were, and put them in my mouth. I didn't swallow them though.

Me: Good. Why not? What stopped you?

Stephanie: I really don't know but I just couldn't do it even though I was really mad.

Me: I see.

Stephanie: I guess I do need therapy huh?

Me: (Smiling). We all have situations where we don't see a way out which often pushes us to the limit. When pushed to the limit we try to figure out how to get out.

Sometimes "getting out" means suicide. You don't have to feel strange for thinking of a way out of your pain. We all look for ways to get out. Some of us overeat, some use drugs or alcohol, and you just happened to think of suicide. But I'm glad you didn't do it because I think there are better options for you. You're very intuitive and smart so I think you are right, therapy will be useful for you. How about we schedule the next session where I can spend 30 minutes with your parents and then the final 30 minutes with you?

Stephanie: That sounds okay to me.

As you can see, I used empathy (i.e., the ability to relate to someone and express understanding of their pain without judging or psychoanalyzing) to connect with her and normalize a very real experience. I also tried my hardest not to address the parents concern over her dating a boy selling drugs. That wasn't the time for me to educate or point out the problem. All I needed to do was listen to her and validate her feelings without condoning the behaviors. I've learned over time that empathizing with a teen who is suicidal causes them to remove their "walls" and barriers so that they can be helped. Most adolescents don't want to be told what to do, unfortunately. They need someone to be a "team player" with them.

Practice with Stephanie

Now it's your turn.

Instructions: Imagine Stephanie is your teen and you need to address her about finding pills in her room. You want to be caring and empathic but you are angry as well. How would you address this situation? Please use the prompts below to help you create and practice an empathic conversation. Add your responses and reactions in the blank areas for parent.

Scenario: Imagine you and Stephanie had an argument 4 days ago about the boy she has been dating. You are her parent and you don't see this boy as being a healthy influence on her. You go to her room and notice she is in the bathroom. You walk around and look at some of the things she has hanging up in her room. You notice a bottle of pills that say "Ritalin" and you know this drug is for ADHD and can only be prescribed by a doctor. You begin to feel your anger rise and you want to quickly inform her that you know she has been using pills. You open the bottle and see that all 30 of the pills looking as if she attempted to take them but removed them from her mouth. Your heart sinks as you begin to suspect she was attempting suicide. Stephanie comes out of the bathroom and finds you holding the bottle of pills. Stephanie addresses you with anger and begins to yell at you about the pills.

How can you make this encounter peaceful and facilitate a greater understanding between the two of you?

Stephanie: WHAT ARE YOU DOING IN MY ROOM? YOU DON'T BELONG IN HERE WITHOUT MY PERMISSION!!!! GET OUT!!!!

Parent:_____
_____
_____
_____
_____
_____
_____

Stephanie: Well...you have no right to be in here. Why are you in my room?

Parent:_____

_____
_____
_____
_____

Stephanie: I know you don't want me with him but I didn't think you would snoop around in my room though. You don't trust me so you think you can just sneak into my room and look at my stuff!

Parent:_____

_____
_____
_____
_____

Stephanie: Can't you see that I am still very angry with you? I haven't come downstairs at all in the past 4 days. Do you even care?

Parent:_____

_____
_____
_____

Stephanie: I don't get why you don't like him so I thought I would just die. There's no way you're going to let me date anyone else like him so I should probably die.

Parent:_____

_____
_____
_____
_____

Stephanie: I don't want to live. I've never felt this way before but I think I might love him.

Parent:_____

_____
_____
_____
_____

Stephanie: Did you ever feel this way before? It's terrible. You like someone then your parents hate them. Your friends like them but then your teachers don't. It makes me feel like I can't make good decisions for myself.

Parent:_____

_____
_____
_____
_____
_____
_____

Stephanie: Well...I don't really want to die. In the moment I thought I did. But I didn't swollow any pills because I guess I was just mad.

Parent:_____

_____
_____
_____
_____
_____
_____

Stephanie: I got those pills from Danny (the boyfriend) by the way. He had them in his room and I stole them after we got into an argument. He was angry with me for taking them.

Parent:_____

_____
_____
_____

Stephanie: He didn't want to get in trouble if I would kill myself. He takes those pills to help him in school.

Parent:_____

_____

_____

_____

_____

Stephanie: Will I be grounded for any of this? I have plans this weekend and don't want to be here!

Parent:_____

_____

_____

_____

_____

Stephanie: I will call or text you throughout the night. Can I still go?

Parent:_____

_____

_____

_____

_____

_____

Stephanie: Ok.

How did you do with this activity? Were you able to respond with empathy without coming across as condescending, patronizing, or authoritarian? You certainly want to maintain control of these kind of encounters and ensure that both you and your teen are making progress during the encounter. Stephanie may still try to argue or manipulate you but your goal, as the parent and adult, is to maintain control over how the conversation progresses. There will certainly be times when you will lose control of your emotions which will result in Stephanie getting more angry with you. But always have the goal of re-centering the conversation and staying on track. Your goal is to help Stephanie understand your concerns while also helping her see you love and care about her. A conversation in which empathy is at the foundation will entail the parent sometimes taking the low road and avoiding further conflict. You can always come back to the conversation at a later time when both you and your teen are calm.

As you will see in the coming examples there are ways to address your concerns with your teen without being authoritarian.

My first meeting with Stephanie's parents

Let's now meet Kimberly and Steve (Stephanie's parents). This is an example of an encounter I had with Stephanie's parents. This example can also be helpful in showing you how a typical conversation goes about a teen who is contemplating suicide.

Me: Hi Kimberly and Steve my name is Tamara. How are you?

Kimberly/Steve: Fine thank you.

Kimberly: Our daughter met with us for a bit while we waited for you and she said she likes you.

Me: Oh wow! That's great. She's a tough one but very insightful and open. I think we're going to do good together.

Kimberly/Steve: That's good to know.

Steve: She really is a good kid, she just got hooked up with the wrong crowd.

Me: I can see that. I told her I think her need for that boy was more emotional than anything.

Kimberly/Steve: Yes! We agree.

Kimberly: We think she's tired of being the only teen girl in her school without a boyfriend. Summer is coming and many of her friends are getting ready to spend the summer with their boyfriends. She never liked being singled out and is still that way.

Me: I see. I wouldn't doubt that is in there somewhere. I noticed while talking to her that she provided very little eye contact

Steve: I agree. She has always been this way.

Me: Let's try using empathy, especially if she shares her suicidal thoughts with you both, and see what happens. Let's schedule our next session.

Kimberly/Steve: That would be great. Thank you so much.

Me: I think we should keep our eyes open but I don't think she is actively suicidal. I would remove any items or pills, however, to maintain safety and prevent an event that may warrant a crisis call.

Kimberly/Steve: Yes. Agree. Thank you

I ended up spending almost a year with this family, even after Stephanie completed probation. Stephanie ended up separating from the boy and moving into another neighborhood which resulted in her going to another school. Although this boy tried to text and Snap-Chat her, she refused his advances after discussing red-flags she missed in multiple sessions with me. Family sessions included me providing psycho-education, encouraging insight-building, and modeling empathic responses. There were times when the family would leave sessions very angry with each other. But these became less and less as both Kimberly and Steve learned to respond to Stephanie's anger using empathy. Empathy had a soothing effect on Stephanie's rages and emotional outbursts. With the inclusion of 2 individual sessions per week for management of suicidal thoughts, 1 family session per week to teach skills, 5 days a week group therapy to build insight, and medication management to control her emotions, she was able to stabilize and reduce the number of therapy sessions and medication meetings with the psychiatrist to 2 times per month. The next challenge for the family and I was getting the school on board.

What teachers can do to help

Teachers are often in a vulnerable place because they often have minimal information about a student. Despite the adolescent spending almost the entire day at school, teachers often only know what they are told, what they hear from other parents and/or students, and their own observations of the family. Teachers can benefit from knowing how a student is really doing by the parent staying in communication with them or by giving them permission (by signing consent) to speak with a teen's therapist. The person, within the school, who would most likely initiate communication with the teen's therapist or treatment team would be the school counselor or school psychologist.

Below I have listed a few ways teachers can reach out to teen's and their families when they become aware that there is a problem:

- **Don't panic:** The last thing teens want to see is an adult, primarily an authority figure like a teacher, panic when they are caught or share suicidal thoughts. It is understandable that an adult would be shocked by a teen admitting that they are suicidal, but we must control our reactions. Controlling our reactions displays to the teen that we are in control, they are not in trouble, and that someone needs to address the issue sooner than later. Demonstrating that we are able to control our emotions as adults can also serve as a model for how adolescents should behave. It also sends the message that you can discuss the issue with them as if they are mature and responsible.

- **Determine how (or if) you should inform the parent(s):** Sometimes those of us who work with teens have to decide if informing a parent of certain things is necessary. For example, a teen divulging to a teacher that they are dating a boy in a higher grade may not be something that a teacher should inform the parent of. However, a teen who reports they are having suicidal thoughts, have a concrete plan, and high level of intent needs to know that their parent will likely be contacted. The parent should be contacted by phone if possible. But other methods of contact could be emailing the parent or sending a letter and even faxing if the parent has one. The teacher would want to document every form of contact they have made for their records, even their attempts to contact a parent. The biggest challenge in situations where teens are suicidal is determining if teachers should inform a parent right away or wait and if it is decided a parent should be informed, what should and should not be said. This will be 90% based on state ethics and laws including the ethics and laws of the teaching profession and 10% based on the relationship the teacher has with the teen and/or family. Teachers will also want to determine when the call should be made or the letter/email/fax should be sent. I suggest as soon as possible after a phone call has been attempted. Before the phone call is attempted a teacher/school administrator should discuss the issue with the teen and explain a call is being made. Everyone should be on the same page. However, if the teen is in opposition to the call, you will want to make it known that teachers are bound by law and must report any incident/event/occurrence that may place the teen in harm's way. You will want to document this discussion and any other discussions the teacher has with the teen.

- **Suggest a "step-down program:"** Once the teen's parent has been contacted it may be helpful for teachers or the school to suggest the family pursue treatment and ask about a program that can help assist the adolescent when he or she has to return to school. For example, a Therapeutic Staff Support (TSS), Behavior Specialist, or another kind of Mobile Therapist may be helpful in supporting the teen's transition back to school if they have been hospitalized or away from school for some time. In my state there are such things as "step-down" programs where a teen is able to go for further therapeutic care if returning home or to school is not in the best interest of the teen. For example, a teen who has been hospitalized for 2-3 weeks due to frequent suicidal thoughts and attempts will most likely fail if released back home or to school right away. In these cases, a hospital may suggest a "step-down program" (that is a program that offers therapy outside of the hospital) which will permit the teen to continue therapy (and perhaps even school) in a therapeutic program designed to prepare teens for returning to their communities. When I worked in a 28-day residential program for children and adolescents, I encountered many clients who were being referred to me following hospitalization. The hospital recognized the child or teen was not fully prepared to return home or school but was no longer in need of hospital services. As a result, the client would come to me and I would provide weekly individual, family, and group therapy in a residential atmosphere where the teen would also attend school. There are also other programs such as partial hospitalization programs where teens are able to return home but must attend a community-based program where they obtain both therapy and school services in the same building.

- **Follow up, follow up, follow up:** I cannot reiterate enough the importance of following up with a parent if a teen has been admitted to a hospital. It will not always be easy for teachers to find out what is going on or to even reach the parent. In these cases, it will be helpful to send a letter or email to the family to check-in. This not only protects the teen and ensure he or she is receiving appropriate care but also helps to build the relationship between the family and the school system. I suggest teachers follow up with a family at least within 12-24hours of finding out about a suicidal teen, offer support or help, offer to speak with the teen's therapist to coordinate care and explain expectations or even set goals for maintaining grades/schoolwork. If it is difficult to reach the family by phone or email, I suggest a teacher, Principal, or school counselor/psychologist send a letter to make some kind of contact.

- **Use brain science to reach teens:** When I work with suicidal teens I try to figure out how I can best reach them. Sometimes I can reach them through rapport building using games, similar interests, or self-disclosure. Other times I have to be more strategic and that's when I turn to brain science. Right-brained kids tend to be more artistic, musical, "free-spirited," creative, spontaneous, and intuitive. These teens can greatly benefit from connecting with an adult who can appeal to these things. A school counselor who can engage the teen in art therapy, music therapy, or deep conversations about life would greatly benefit the teen. Left-brained teens are often more logical, detailed, analytical, and focused on rules. These kids will benefit from completing therapeutic worksheets or journaling about their thoughts and feelings. Because most adolescents struggle with trusting adults and sharing their thoughts and feelings with them, it is important to figure out how best to connect with them and maintain a caring, open relationship. Sometimes targeting their strengths and interests is the best way to connect. When I meet with teens who are right-brained, I have them journal to me or share their artistic abilities and interest in music. It is both a rapport building and bonding experience. For left-brained teens, I will engage them in discussion or in completing therapeutic worksheets. Most left-brained kids are able to analyze things, explore them, and process feelings by writing things down in detailed or bullet-like points. Left-brained kids are also able to hold conversations with adults and engage in weighing the pros and cons of their decisions, concerns, or behaviors. I love engaging left-brained teens in discussions and worksheets. The feedback I get from left-brained teens is amazing and sometimes we end of discussing existential topics such as the purpose of life, the usefulness of altruism, etc.

- **Be lenient and understanding:** It is important that teachers allow a family to "recover" and heal. Once a teen has reported suicidal thoughts and has begun receiving treatment, time to heal, recuperate, and refocus is very important. If a teen is bombarded with things too soon, they are likely to "relapse" into old patterns of thinking and behaving. This is why a safety/crisis plan will be one of the most important tools teachers and parents will use (discussed in chapter 6).

- **Offer to connect with the teen's treatment team:** Teachers should reach out to the family and offer to speak with the teen's therapist or treatment team to ensure a smooth transition back to school if the teen has been out of school for some time.

- **Carefully weigh the pros and cons of losing rapport:** It is possible that once a teacher finds out that a teen is suicidal, and sets out to inform the parent, that the teen shuts down completely. All rapport may be lost as teens may conceptualize this as "turning on them," "going against them," or "betraying trust." Teens have very fragile egos and sense of self and feels as though they have lost the confidence or trust of an adult in an important role (i.e., a teacher, parent, principal, etc.), can lead to depression or anxiety and ultimately a return of suicidal thoughts. Teachers should take time to weigh the pros and cons of informing parents of a teen's suicidal thoughts and in involving themselves in the teen's treatment. Weighing the pros and cons should happen as soon as possible so that if a teen is in imminent danger they can get help sooner than later. Once a decision has been made, a teacher or another administrator from the school should inform the teen of the plan and attempt to get them on board for talking about the issue with a parent. The conversation can occur before school, while the teen is still in school, or after school. The process of having to inform the parent of what has been found out should be compassionate, caring, and empathic. The teen should never feel as if they are in trouble or will be punished. A teacher should ensure the teen understands why informing the parent is important.

In some cases where the teen is not in imminent danger and denies having a suicide plan, the teen may be mature and honest enough to inform their parents of what happened in school and why. In these cases, I suggest entrusting the teen to tell their parent(s) about the suicidal thoughts before the teacher calls the parent. I suggest the teacher call the parent an hour or so after school to follow up. This approach should only be used in cases where the teen has denied they will harm themselves or others, is mature and responsible and has a stable household with responsible parents. In cases where these things are lacking, I suggest the teen not be allowed to leave school without calling the parent. Although this can feel like punishment and be very embarrassing to the teen, the goal is not to appease them but to ensure they are safe. The process, again, does not have to occur as if the teen is in trouble but should communicate concern and support.

Putting it all together

It is important for all adults in the lives of adolescents to support them in whatever way possible. Adolescents not only struggle with their self-esteem, emotions, and thought patterns, but also trusting adults and expressing themselves to them. Because of this, it will be very important that parents and teachers learn how to connect and communicate with teens. One way to communicate with your teen would be to figure out what kind of a brain they have. Are they left-brained or right-brained? Are they creative and artistic, or logical and analytical? Once you narrow down what type of brain the teen has, you stand a better chance of figuring out how best to connect. For your right-brained teen, you may be able to connect with them over music, art, poetry, dance, or some other form of creative thinking. For your left-brained teen, you may find that discussing the problem in private will be enough to help them figure out what they need. Whatever way you choose to connect with the teen, it is important that you consider other ways to support them such as by pursuing mental health treatment, the right kind of therapist, and/or medication management.

Sample letter to the school

(School address here)

(attn: name of person letter is going to)

Re: (student first name, last initial)

Dear (school employee),

I am (student's name) mother/father and would like to inform you of a serious matter reported to me by my daughter on (date). My daughter reported having suicidal thoughts and writing a suicide letter on (date). She has an appointment with an outpatient therapist on (date) at (time) for an assessment. I have enclosed a copy of the clinic's release of information form for you to sign in the event you would like to reach out to her therapist. You may also contact me at (number) in the event you would need to.

Thank you very much,

(parent name)

Enclosure (attach the consent form from the clinic if you have one)

NOTES

CHAPTER 5

Pursuing Mental Health Treatment

"Tell me and I forget, teach me and I may remember, involve me and I learn."

- Benjamin Franklin

If you had to pursue mental health treatment for your teen would you know what to do? Would you know where to turn? Would you feel informed and confident with what you know? If not, join the millions of Americans who feel similarly. Sadly, there isn't a lot of information available to parents, families, or even teachers because they are a "special" population. What I mean by this is that many parents, families, and teachers are put on the back-burner when it comes to being educated to mental illness and teen suicide. For all teens over the age of 14, information is given to them as the "patient" or "client" and rarely given to the parent without consent from the patient/client. Some parents have to play the "middle man" between the mental health system and the educational system to ensure both systems are collaborating. Other parents simply don't know what to do as some therapists rarely if ever make contact with them or a teen's school if they are pursuing treatment. The process of integrating both systems can feel impossible.

The topic of suicide has been a taboo topic in our society for decades and still remains buried beneath other topics involving teens such as teen sex, teen pregnancy, or dating. But for most adolescents in today's society, the topic of suicide is no longer taboo for them. In fact, most teens talk openly among each other about suicide more so than they do with their parents. This means that the adults in their lives must broach the topic and do it in a way that makes teens feel comfortable and accepted. I have learned over time that most teens considering suicide are delicate and we must be careful in how we approach the topic, evaluate the situation, and offer suggestions or comments meant to be supportive. Some comments, suggestions, or questions can do more harm than good. So it is important that we examine how to strategically address teens, obtain the correct treatment, and find and maintain natural or community supports. The first step for you is figuring out who to see for help.

Who to see for mental health treatment

Some parents have major concerns about pursuing mental health treatment because of stigma, preconceived or inaccurate views, and confusion over who to seek for help. Would you know who to talk to and what to do to get things started? There are many parents who struggle with getting their teen involved in mental health care. One of the reasons is because mental health care can be confusing. As a result of all of the various levels of care and criteria needing to be met in order to be admitted to a treatment program, some parents avoid it all together and simply talk to their family doctor. In some ethnic minority cultures (primarily the African American and Native American cultures), parents tend to find support in their communities in local churches, health clubs, or support groups. But I strongly believe that you, as the parent, should know what the letters next to a healthcare provider's last name actually means. Although this is not a guarantee of professional service, not knowing a provider's credentials can be dangerous in the long-run. I have heard horror stories about parents who trusted a "professional" because they claimed to be credentialed, only to later find out they had absolutely no idea of what they were doing.

Below I offer a few examples of professional titles you may come across while pursuing mental health treatment:

PCP – Primary Care Physician: A primary care physician may be your family practitioner or medical doctor (MD). These doctors see teens for check-ups, prescribe medication, request tests, etc. from the medical perspective. A PCP's main focus is to care for the body, not the mind per se. However, families can still ask their PCP for a referral to a mental health professional. Some medical doctors are often willing to start medication until they can make a referral to someone who can help a family struggling with mental health challenges. If your teen is suicidal and shares suicidal thoughts with the PCP, the doctor is likely to recommend an appointment with a local clinic to see a therapist or psychiatrist. PCP's play an important role in referring to mental health providers. One reason is because most families prefer to discuss challenges their teen may be having with a healthcare provider who is less stigmatizing than a mental health provider. Another reason is because some families do not know who to turn to.

MD – Medical Doctor/Psychiatrist: A psychiatrist is also a medical doctor with a specialization in mental health care. Psychiatrists will be able to consider both the medical and mental health perspective of your teen. A psychiatrist will most likely monitor for need of medication and refer you to a therapist for counseling. Although some provide therapy, their main role is medication management. Some teens have reported feeling that their psychiatrist is unable to relate to them or engage them in comfortable conversation. The style of the psychiatrist you meet will depend on a lot of different components such as culture and age, gender, work and life experiences, and education. I encourage you to search around and to avoid settling because it is easy. You want your teen to have someone that they can connect with, respect, and appreciate.

LPC – Licensed Professional Counselor: A licensed professional counselor is a mental health professional with over 5 years of schooling and possibly a lot of training. Every LPC is different. I am an LPC and had 5 years of higher education in a graduate program in counseling psychology. I also have 10 years experience in the field in multiple capacities. I have worked in RTF's, clinics, hospitals, schools, delinquency centers, community mental health centers, research universities, and now group-based private practice. Some LPC's have had more or less training than I have had. A licensed professional must have about 3,000 hours (3years) of counseling experience/practice under the supervision of a seasoned licensed professional in the state in which the LPC resides. Someone with a PhD or PsyD can also have an LPC in their state. Some states might have strict or less strict rules. It all depends on where you live and the state law.

LCSW – Licensed Clinical Social Worker: A LCSW is a mental health professional with about the same (or slightly less) number of years in higher education and training as an LPC. The process is about the same as that of an LPC. The only difference is that some claim LCSW's may have a slightly different focus on psychological pathology than LPC's. Many LCSW's have strong skills in community mental health services.

PhD./PsyD. - Psychologist: A PhD. or PsyD. mental health professional does the same exact work as an LPC or LCSW. The only real difference is that they can conduct research on mental health conditions, lead research studies, and also provide personality tests such as the MMPI (Minnesota Multiphasic Personality Inventory). The MMPI assesses personality traits and provides a score that helps psychologists, police forces, and other professionals identify (and sometimes rule out) individuals who may exhibit sociopathic personality traits. A PsyD. And/or PhD. both have a bit more schooling (somewhere around 5-7 years).

All of these credentialed professionals may be certified or have special training. No two healthcare providers are the same, even if they have the same credentials or went to the same school for their degree. No matter who you choose as your teen's mental health provider, it is important that you carefully choose who you want your teen to see. An important concept to stand by is the fact that the degree or experience doesn't count as much as the style, personality, and fit of the provider. Teens should feel comfortable after a few sessions and be able to engage with the therapist in a healthy fashion. I suggest that parents attend at least 2-3 sessions with the teen before letting them meet with the therapist alone. This ensures that the therapist is appropriate, the teen feels comfortable, and that you get some of your questions answered. Although the therapeutic style of the therapist should be respected, you can ask the therapist if you can sit in on a few sessions with your teen present before your teen goes solo.

What not to say to teens you are trying to get into treatment

Talking to teenagers can be one of the most difficult things to do as a parent, therapist, and teacher because some teens are defensive, argumentative, oppositional, and challenging. Some are easygoing, understanding, wise beyond their years, and intuitive. But for the most part, teenagers struggle with listening to their parents and embrace their wisdom. Thankfully, I have had clinical experiences and opportunities to learn why some teens are so difficult to reach and hard to guide. In most cases, the ways in which adults broach topics, when, and how has a lot to do with a teen's defensiveness. It is important that we, as adults, find strategic and authentic ways to relate to teens who may be considering suicide. As stated in the previous chapter, teens who feel judged or criticized may completely shut-down and refuse to talk. It is our job to figure out how to "reach" them. It is not, however, fair that we, as adults, endure disrespect or displacement of angry feelings while trying to help them. Teens need to be reminded to remain respectful at all times. But we also need to figure out how best to reach them. Below are a few examples of statements (I have heard throughout my career) from family members of teens considering suicide. These are the very statements you want to strive to avoid when broaching or facilitating a conversation about suicide with your teen:

- **"You have so much to be thankful for:"** The last thing your teen, who is considering suicide, wants to hear is "but look at all the things you have...." When we are hurting and want the emotional, psychological, and sometimes physical pain to stop, we look for a way to end it. For many teens who internalize their emotions, they have become "experts" in burying their pain in under age drinking, using drugs, gambling, sexual promiscuity, etc. But for the other percentage of teens who do not do these things, suicide may appear to be less harmful and painful at the time. It isn't the best option but we cannot blame them for considering it. Minimizing the problem by making the above statement can actually do more harm than good by making them isolate and feel ashamed. Remember, the goal is not to chastise, intimidate, or judge your teen. Your job and my job is to figure out how to help, how to get the teen to talk, and how to relate in a way that makes them feel safe enough to talk.

- **"Why would you ever consider such a thing?"** In some cases, when a teen shares they are considering suicide communication can become strained because of the automatic emotions that arise in the teen and the adult. As a result, some adults will ask questions or make statements that really don't help the situation. Statements such as: "why would you ever consider such a thing?" can result in the teen feeling ashamed, stupid, or "crazy" for feeling the way they do. This can send an indirect message that their feelings are strange, abnormal, or unimportant.

- **"Did you know only weak people think of suicide?"** I once had a 15 year old client who shared his suicidal thoughts in a group therapy session focused on disclosure and building rapport between the members. My client, who was being seen by me when I was an intern, decided to share his deepest thoughts about suicide which included how he would stage his death, kill himself, and then "rest eternally." A group member, who displayed avoidant and narcissistic personality traits, decided that was the time to say "did you know only weak people think of suicide?" That was my client's final day of group therapy and he refused to return. This young man struggled not only with similar comments from his family and friends, but now from a therapeutic group setting. Thankfully I was able to give him a call and encourage him to pursue individual therapy. He stayed in contact with me as he participated in therapy through a different agency. After 2 years of CBT treatment and medication management, he came back to my agency to share a list of ways his family and friends (including his co-group members) reduced his ability to progress. It is very important that we strive to be balanced, authentic, and careful in how we talk to those considering suicide.

- **"You're unstable right now.** Do you think you need help?" How difficult would it be for you to accept your parent making this statement to you? Would you get angry, more depressed, and/or discouraged? Or would you accept this statement as supportive and caring? Depending on how a person would pose this question would determine how you would respond. A change in tone of voice, attitude, or mood can make all the difference. Be careful in how you ask questions and follow-up questions. Body language and eye contact is especially important with teens.

- **"You should never mention suicide.** That is depressing:" An adult making this type of statement would really concern me. Teens should always feel comfortable discussing their deepest feelings and challenges with the adults they care about the most. Parents should avoid making statements that may make the teen feel like the "gloom and doom" person of the family. This statement would be reckless and uncaring.

- **"Don't think like that:"** In some cases where families remain secretive, emotionally distant, and dismissive, statements like this are very likely to occur. In fact, in homes where abuse and trauma exist, these statements are likely to occur on a frequent basis, especially if the home climate encourages internalized emotions. I encourage you, as the parent, to avoid this statement. There are more appropriate ways you can get your point across. Something like "please don't think like that Lily, I love you" would be caring and warm. A statement such as "don't think like that, that's bad" could make a teen feel guilty for experiencing strong emotions.

- **"Get over it:"** It is also important to be careful in the ways in which you may try to encourage your teen to move on into their future. In some cases, because of fear or uncertainty on how to handle a suicidal teen, an adult may insinuate or subliminally state that the teen should "get over" or "move on" past a painful thing/situation/experience that is making them feel suicidal. "Getting over it" is often easier said than done in many cases. A parent saying "get over it" is likely to push the teen to consider suicide as the best option available to them. When suicidal teens feel unheard or misunderstood, they are likely to become depressed and overwhelmed which are two ingredients for suicide. Feeling misunderstood, unloved, or dismissed are often the very emotions that trigger suicidal thinking.

- **"Grow up:"** I have heard family members make this statements during intense family sessions in which a teen is struggling with suicidal thoughts. These kind of sessions can resemble an "intervention meeting" in which family members challenge the teen to "grow up" or "get serious." These kind of statements can do more harm than good. Again, these kind of statements often "push" suicidal youths more toward suicide as they may begins to feel unheard, burdened, and beat up on. There are better ways to coerce a teen to mature and make more sound decisions. A statement such as: "I see you are struggling at this time and anyone in your shoes would. I just believe that if you continue to hold on that you will find peace. If you let us support you, you will be okay. It may not feel you will get past this now, but with maturity and experience comes peace and understanding" would be more appropriate.

- **"You are trying to manipulate others:"** It is true that some teens use suicidal gestures, attempts, and statements to control others, primarily those they are in a personal relationship with (i.e., parent, boyfriend, marriage, family, co-worker, etc). Some teens with borderline personality traits will use suicide to control others and get their emotional needs met. Some will also use suicide to manipulate or control as well, especially when the teen does not get their way or is being asked to meet a specific expectation. While working in a juvenile delinquency center and school-based program for kids on probation, I had 4 clients who met criteria for BPD but due to age, was unable to have the diagnosis. However, this did not stop me from using tools used to treat BPD. While engaging my 14-year-old female client in a session focused on emotion regulation and distress tolerance, she admitted to using dramatic behaviors, tears, and suicidal gestures as a way to "get my way" and "control my boyfriend." During a session with my 14-year-old female client focused on emotion regulation, she admitted to using dramatic behaviors, tears, and suicidal gestures as a way to "get my way" and "control my boyfriend." If you are noticing a pattern of attention-seeking behavior by using suicidal gestures or statements, pursuing therapy will be helpful for not only the teen but for you, as the parent, as well. You will need to learn tools for responding to an emotionally labile teen who uses suicidal statements to control.

- **"Stop acting this way:"** Sadly, I have witnessed some parents speak to their teenager in this way in family sessions. There is a degree of denial and fear within this statement. "Stop acting this way" may be a statement a parent uses if they observe their teen struggling with symptoms they have never seen before. It is frightening for a parent to learn of problematic thinking patterns, behaviors, or feelings that they cannot remedy themselves. As a result, it is not uncommon, for example, that a parent respond to a suicidal teen by stating "stop acting this way, we did not raise you to be like this." Suicidal thoughts have very little to do with how a teen is raised and has more to do with an illness that needs treatment. It is important to keep this in mind and to begin to refrain from making statements that may place blame.

It is important, as stated in chapter 3, that you learn how to relate to, connect with, and help your teen who is in desperate need of your support and understanding. You will want to display empathy, active listening (i.e., truly focusing on what the teen is saying without being distracted), and compassion at all times. It's sometimes the only key to the locked heart of a teen.

Exercise activity

Below is an exercise that will help you practice a better way to communicate with your teen about their suicidal thoughts. The prompts will help you move through the exercise a bit easier. You can certainly go back to chapter 3 and the beginning of this chapter to remind yourself of what we have learned so far. Please write down your answers on the lines provided.

Parent: Hi Steph, how was school today?

Stephanie: Good. I didn't see Danny today. That should make you happy.

Parent: Oh Steph. You know I want the best for you because....

_____
_____
_____
_____

Stephanie: I know. I know. You say that all the time.

Parent: Would you have a minute to talk?....

_____
_____
_____
_____
_____

Stephanie: Am I in trouble again!?

Parent:_____
_____
_____

_____

_____

Stephanie: Great. Cause I was about to get angry and say...

Parent: No. You've been doing so mcuh better in school and at home which is why I want to talk to you about hanging out with negative peers including Danny. I know you like him but I am your parent and my job is to

_____

_____

_____

_____

_____

Stephanie: Ok. Will we be done in the next hour because I'm meeting with Kelly for homework?

Parent: Of course. But we need to talk. I have been thinking about at a few things regarding your past suicide attempt and your attempt to seriously harm yourself by cutting.

I feel that you get so overwhelmed with everything that you_____

_____

_____

_____

_____but I don't want you to feel_____

_____

_____

_____

_____

Parent: Do you feel that way when I bring this topic up?

Stephanie: A little bit. I mean because you won't let it go and I'm stuck trying not to get mad at you. I told you I didn't want to talk about this anymore.

Parent: I understand that but...

_____

_____

_____

_____

_____

_____.You can't reject support because of your fear of being found out by others. There are definitely other teens who are getting help for similar reasons. You're not the only teen who needs to talk to someone. Would you be willing to see a therapist for support?

Stephanie: A therapist?! For what?

Parent:_____
_____
_____
_____

____.I saw a therapist when I was your age. It was actually pretty fun because all I did was talk about me. I would also get suggestions or advice that my peers couldn't give me. So...what do you think? Will you give it a try?

Stephanie: Okay, if I must. But this therapist must be cool. I don't want an old lady trying to tell me what to do. I hate that.

Parent: Of course Steph. I just want you to be safe and happy. Having suicidal thoughts and wanting to cut must be a lonely place to be. I truly believe you can benefit from_____
_____
_____
_____

Parent: If you don't like it, we can move on to another one or take a break for a while. Do you want to help me make the phone call or at least be here when I schedule the appointment?

Stephanie: Sure. Why not.

Parent: Thank you Steph for cooperating and considering further help. I'm so proud of you.

How did you do with this activity?

Were you able to write down healthy examples of things you could say to your teen? The goal of this exercise is to help you explore what you could say to keep things calm and focused. Talking to your teen isn't the only person you will have to talk to at this stage. You will also have to reach out to healthcare providers who can offer you and your teen help. A few frequently asked questions on the first appointment with a therapist are listed below. I encourage you to make a list of questions that you may want to ask your teen's therapist during the first appointment.

Questions to ask on first appointments

I'm sure you are just as nervous as your teen when it comes to attending the very first session. One way to reduce anxiety is to come up with a few questions, with your teen, prior to the session. Here is a list of possible questions to ask on your first appointment:

Will there be individual and family therapy? If so, what will that consist of?

In many cases, clients often feel around in the dark when seeking a therapist. They are uninformed about the various types of therapists there are and the various types of training that certain therapists have received. The type of training a therapist has often influences the type of therapy you will receive. It may be difficult to identify what is called a therapist's *theoretical orientation*. A theoretical orientation or theoretical framework includes a therapist's background, worldview, work experience, therapeutic tools, and training that influences a therapists way he or she engages with a client. Asking a therapist what type of therapy they will use with your teen is a great first step. There are ways you can ask this question without coming right out and saying "so what will you do to help my teen?" This can be perceived as pushy and domineering. You want to be careful how you pose this question. You will also have to listen closely as some therapists may discuss their approach using language you may not fully understand. You will have to ask what "school of thought" (or theoretical orientation) the therapist uses. For example, I use a trauma-informed, CBT, person-centered, and existential approach with my clients. There are times I rely on one of the above more depending on what my client's need is for the day. For example, if a teen comes to therapy crying and stating that they have been expelled from school because of repeated suicide attempts on school grounds, I will use a person-centered, existential approach focusing on showing compassion and empathy while helping the teen process their emotions and thoughts, understand their triggers, identify the consequences and better ways to cope with stress in the future. Some therapists are "eclectic" which means that they use a variety of approaches to treat teens. I encourage you to be very cautious of this approach as it has been very controversial in the field of psychotherapy. You don't want to buy the service and regret it later.

What is your policy on social media and communicating with you there?

Some therapists, like me, have social media sites that have a specific purpose that may be unrelated to the therapy itself. For example, I have a blog but I also have a website, twitter page, Pinterest, and a host of other social media sites to reach various audiences around the world. Although I have a social media policy, I do not, however, allow my clients to interact with me there and ask personal questions. Some therapists prefer their client not to explore their social media sites at all. You want to be sure you understand what your teen's therapist prefers because if your teen crosses a boundary they can possibly destroy the therapeutic relationship or cause the therapist to reiterate their boundaries. Some teens may interpret this as embarrassing or even hurtful.

How long are sessions and can my teen see you more than once a week?

Most parents and teens are uninformed about how therapy works. Therapy has rules (some spoken and some unspoken) that help the relationship grow in a therapeutic fashion. It's appropriate to ask your teen's therapist how often they can see your teen and in what ways can you contact them throughout the week. I offer parents the opportunity of calling me throughout the week if they need something or have a concern. I have a 24 to 72-hour return call policy. This means that if a parent chooses to leave a voicemail or email/text me, I will respond within 24-72 hours after receiving their message. Some therapists, however, prefer clients to contact them throughout the week via email or write concerns/questions down and discuss them during the next session. Other therapists, especially for teens over the age of 14 limits contact with the parent in order to grow a relationship of trust with the teen. Every therapist is different. You want to learn how your teen's therapist operates by asking to sit in on a session, asking questions, and initiating communication when necessary. Word of mouth or the therapist's website is a great way to learn more about the therapist's style. But most therapists have no problem talking to you about their approach.

How do you view human suffering?

It may be helpful to you to keep your eyes open for clues on how your teen's therapist may view human suffering.

It may be awkward for you to come right out and ask this question. So I discourage it. But I do encourage you to look for clues. A therapist's worldview has the potential of coming out in sessions. Some therapists are overly positive, some are overly pessimistic, and others are balanced in their view of life. It's perfectly okay to ask your teen about their therapist and how they feel about the therapist's view of things. You can say something like "Steph, how was therapy today? Do you find yourself connecting with your therapist's view of what you're going through?" Other therapists may simply offer this information during the first session. This is the approach I tend to take. I explain that my life perspective is what drives my therapy approach, attitude, and perception. My theoretical orientation or approach to treatment is further cemented by my personal belief system of human suffering. Because I integrate both CBT (Cognitive Behavior Therapy) and existential principles, I see human suffering as an inevitable part of life that can be coped with by adopting a balanced and faith-based perspective infused with behavioral techniques such as using coping skills, using mindfulness meditation, and breathing techniques. My approach to human suffering also includes using other tools helpful tools such as prayer, community involvement, self-care, changing imbalanced thoughts and perceptions, journaling, and relaxation training. Other therapists believe that you have the power to control every aspect of your life if you just try hard enough. Still, other therapists believe things that perhaps you would totally disagree with. You have the right, as a parent, to ask questions as long as you are kind, modest, and open-minded. You wouldn't want to challenge your teen's therapist in such a way that the therapist is turned off and feels threatened.

Do I pay for sessions before or after?

Some therapists will have this information hanging in the office or written in their office policy. Other therapists simply don't make this clear enough. It's okay to ask if you are to pay for therapy before or after the session and in what ways can you pay. Some technologically astute therapists use PayPal, Square, or a billing platform to assist clients in paying for sessions. But other therapists prefer check or money order only. Everyone is different. You'd be surprised at how many parents ask me how they should pay for sessions. If you want to avoid feeling stressed about payments, feel free to ask.

Will you make contact with my teen's previous treatment provider?

I find it very useful to obtain consent from my client's family and contact previous treatment providers (i.e., psychiatrists, therapists, behavioral specialists, holistic doctors, etc). This process can provide a great deal of information to me about the client. It's often very helpful to obtain historical information that can inform treatment. You also, however, have the right to ask that your previous treatment provider not be contacted if you believe their opinion would not be helpful. If you sign a consent and later want to revoke it, you can call the therapist and inform them that you would like to withdraw your consent. Of course, you cannot do this with a teen who is over the age of 14 because they are legally permitted to make this decision on their own. Talk to your teen about how they feel about their therapist contacting previous providers.

What is your experience with culture and ethnicity?

Some clients, primarily the African American and Native American culture, find it very difficult to trust the therapeutic process. Some not so obvious reasons include the fact that the majority of mental health professionals in today's society are Caucasian and these two ethnic cultures have experienced a long history of violated trust and oppression. It's difficult for this population of clients to trust the very culture that betrayed them for centuries. A skilled therapist with experience working with ethnic minorities is extremely valuable and very much needed in today's society. It is okay to ask how much experience your teen's therapist has with ethnic minority clients. An inner-city youth is not going to open up to a middle-class white male or female about his father's incarceration, his mother's substance abuse, and his truancy. It will be a challenge, to say the least. The teen is likely to feel that his Caucasian therapist will not be able to relate to him or utilize the appropriate tools needed to reach and help him. I have also struggled with certain cultures due to having minimal exposure to them. For example, it wasn't until I began working in rural areas providing psychotherapy that I learned about the special needs of clients living in rural or remote areas. Clients who live in remote areas have "special needs" that not all therapists can cater to. It takes an experienced therapist to identify and treat their specific needs. Don't be afraid to bring this up and ask about experience with different cultures and populations.

What happens if my insurance runs out or insurance stops paying for therapy?

If you use insurance for your teen's therapy you are probably well aware of the fact that sometimes insurance companies change their rules or policies, adjust your deductible, or simply stop paying. Most therapists who accept medical assistance (government-based insurance) or private insurance have to complete what is known as Continued Stay Review. Although this may vary by state and insurance company, the reviews can be brutal. A therapist who has to "prove" a client would benefit from continued treatment will have to call the insurance company and provide reasons for why a client should remain in therapy and why insurance should continue to pay. If your insurance company does not believe treatment is warranted, insurance will stop paying which means your teen's therapist does not get paid for services rendered. You will either have to enter a payment agreement with the therapist which says you will pay out-of-pocket for your teen's therapy or you will have to stop therapy. It is useful to ask your teen's therapist how he or she will handle this process in the event it happens. You can also ask if your teen's therapist offers payment plans to assist you in the event your insurance stops covering sessions or changes.

Who can I contact for emergencies or crisis situations when you are out of the office?

Because the majority of my career has included me working in agencies and hospitals, I have always had someone, during my vacation time, to fill in for me. This is often the case for most therapists, especially those who are not in private practice. However, for those therapists who work in private practice, there is often no one else to fill in for the therapist when they are out of the office. It's a great idea to ask your teen's therapist who you can contact when they are not reachable or available.

There are lots of questions you should ask your teen's therapist. I encourage you to choose questions that are very important to ask and save other questions for a later time. You wouldn't want to overwhelm the therapist.

Understanding levels of mental health treatment

As you can see there are multiple questions that need to be asked during the first session. Some therapists may make little time for questions due to time constraints or an inability to connect with clients. You will have to be slightly assertive with this kind of therapist. Other therapists do a great job of answering questions or scheduling a free consultation before your teen's actual session so that you can have all your questions answered. I encourage you to ask questions so that you can be armed with the appropriate knowledge to plan ahead. But I also encourage you to be kind, patient, and polite in asking questions. You certainly don't want to come across as rude or aggressive. This can destroy a potentially equal and healthy relationship. You want to start off on the right foot.

Sadly, many parents and teachers struggle to understand the levels of mental health care available to suicidal teens. In order for teachers to support parents, they must know what treatment options are available to families. In order for parents to quickly obtain needed services for their adolescent child, they need to know the levels of the mental health system and what it takes to obtain care. Below I discuss a few examples, from my own experience with clients, of various levels of care such as a residential treatment, hospitals, partial programs, and outpatient settings. In the following pages, I will discuss each program as a dialogue to give you an idea of how I assess a teen's need for a specific program.

Residential treatment for suicidal thoughts and behaviors: William

Let's meet "William" and his mother Tiffany. William was a 13-year-old biracial young man who had been involved in therapy services since the age of 5. I met with William and his maternal grandmother, Lisa, for an intake while working in a residential treatment facility (RTF) specifically for children and adolescents. An RTF is very similar to a group home but includes a school as part of the RTF (often on the same grounds). Before I met with William and his grandmother for an intake, I obtained consent from his mother Tiffany so that I could request his medical record from his previous therapist. I faxed over a consent and called to confirm receipt of the fax. The next day I obtained his medical file. William was diagnosed with a severe mental illness and had a long history of oppositional defiant behavior.

He had been treated since the age of 5 for emotion dysregulation (i.e., an inability to control emotions), hallucinations, and rebellious behaviors such as refusing to comply or listen. He was being admitted to the RTF due to multiple failed attempts to keep him at lower levels of care such as in-home therapy and/or outpatient therapy.

RTF was the last option and his mom and grandmother were exhausted.

Me: Hi Lisa and William, my name is Támara and I will be your therapist here in RTF. How are you both?

Lisa/William: Fine. Thank you.

Me: So let me tell you a bit about myself and then I'll ask you more about why RTF is an option for you right now. I am a licensed therapist with about 6 years of experience with children and adolescents with disruptive behavior and mood disorders. That means I work with kids who are struggling with their behavior and who may be depressed or anxious. I am also certified in trauma-informed care, which is a form of therapy used for youngsters who may have experienced a traumatic event in their life. Do you have any questions about this before we move forward?

Lisa: No. Not right now.

William: No. (Nodding).

Me: Great. Can you tell me a bit about why you are here?

Lisa: Well, there has been so much I don't know where to start. But I'll just give you information from age 8.

Me: (Smiling). That's fine. Start wherever you'd like.

Lisa: (Smiling/nervous laughter). Thank you. Tiffany, my daughter, first noticed that something wasn't right when Will would sit straight up in his bed at night and talk as if he was having a conversation with a group of friends. He would do this every night which turned into every single day as well. I don't know what to think but he got so comfortable with doing this that he would talk as if he was talking to a group of people in front of his peers during school. It got so bad that the school encouraged my daughter to seek therapy. She did and that didn't go so well.

Me: Ok. I see. What happened?

Lisa: (Exhaling). Well, he didn't like his therapist and his mother had to force him to go to therapy every week. He would fight, kick, and threaten suicide. I don't think his therapist was a good fit in the first place.

Me: What gender was the therapist? What were the credentials if you can remember?

Lisa: He was a "general therapist" and told us he works with almost everyone.

Me: I see. He was eclectic which means he doesn't specialize in one thing. That can be tricky. Also, there is a possibility that William will respond better to a female, considering that he has been raised by both you and your daughter and hasn't had too many relationships with adult males.

Lisa: Maybe? Okay. I didn't know. I thought a therapist is a therapist. Well, at any rate, my grandson started talking about suicide more and more and then threatened to run out of the house into traffic. My daughter lives on a busy road that leads to the highway.

Me: Oh God. I see.

Lisa: He was getting so bad in his mental health that he ran away 5 times which pushed my daughter to have to call the police. Thankfully Will wasn't arrested. The police just asked him for his address and brought him back home.

Me: That's really sweet of them.

Lisa: Oh yes. I thank God for that. So I guess since this time he has gotten much worse. He now tries to cut himself with anything he can get his hands on. Just last night he tried to hang himself. We can't leave him alone. RTF is our only option right now. We've tried everything else and it failed us.

Me: That's very clear. I'm so sorry. William do you know what an RTF is?

William: (nodding) No.

Me: An RTF is a residential treatment facility that you live in for between 3 months (90 days) to 2 years (24 months) to receive therapy and learn skills on a daily basis. You will see me at least 3 times a week for individual, group, and family therapy. You will live on what's called a "unit" with other kids your age. You will be on an all-boys unit where you will be supervised 24/7 until you are able to be safe again. You will also be able to have visits with your family every Saturday and Sunday as long as your mom or grandma schedules ahead of time with me or the staff on your unit. Make sense?

William: Yeah. Can I play my video games?

Me: Well, that's a tricky one because the staff are very strict on what you can and cannot take on the unit with you. Anything could (and has been) used as a weapon to harm self or others. There may be a PlayStation 2 or X-box on the unit already that you can earn access to for good and safe behavior. Your grandma or mom can also bring your iPad or something like that for you to play with while they are visiting you. Make sense?

William: Yeah. Can I call them too?

Me: Yes. Absolutely. But you have to have permission to call your grandma or mother throughout the day. Kids typically get about 1-2 calls a day at certain times. It can sound scary at first but once you get used to the way things are here, you will be okay. You will also see your family in family sessions each week with me. If you are having a really bad day and need to talk to me, we can also use some of that time to call your grandma or mom.

William: okay. That is good with me. But I'm getting scared I won't get out.

Lisa: I know baby. But your mom and I don't know what else to do. You are not safe at home and I can't have you running out of the house onto the highway to end your life. That would kill me and your mother both. Nothing else is working and so our only hope is to admit you to this program. Please don't be mad at us.

William: I'm not (sad look on his face).

William was a great kid but I struggled to get him to understand the severity of his illness. The first night on the unit he began to talk to imaginary "family members" who had died and come back to "save him" from the RTF. I was called by staff the next day before I got to work because William had tried to swallow soap from the boy's bathroom. I met with William for an individual session to discuss the incident. He did not want to meet with me and refused to come into my office. So I went to him instead. I asked him what was going on and how he slept. He reported, "my dead family members told me to get out of here as soon as possible because I was going to die a terrible and slow death." I remember asking him for details about his symptoms (i.e., hallucinations and delusions) and tried to get him to see that I was on his side. Eventually, the RTF scheduled what is called an ISPT (interagency planning team) meeting which determines how long a client should remain in treatment. He was admitted for another 90 days due to intense suicidal thoughts and suicide attempts complicated by delusions and hallucinations. For teens who are struggling with severe mental illness and require a lot of supervision, the next step in the "hierarchy of mental health treatment" is hospitalization. William was always two steps shy of hospitalization. He was able to avoid it every time he had a crisis. Sadly, he knew what buttons to push with staff and when to "act normal" in order to avoid hospitalization. Sadly, my next client wasn't so lucky.

Hospitalization for suicidal thoughts: Kelsey

Kelsey was a 16 year old Caucasian female from an inner city neighborhood. She lived with both of her parents, Amy and Mike, and her maternal grandmother Bernice. Both of Kelsey's parents were loving and stable. Amy worked part-time as a substitute teacher while her husband worked full time as a server at Starbucks. Because both parents were always working, Bernice offered to "babysit" Kelsey at her house. Eventually the family had to move in with Amy's mother as Amy and Mike's home went into foreclosure. Sadly, Kelsey suffered not only embarrassment for having to move out of her 4 bedroom spacious house, but also feelings of depression and loss. Kelsey grew up in that home and wanted to remain there until admitted to college. Now she was facing having to move out on her own into a dorm in the next 3 years. She was also facing verbal and physical bullying at a new school after her peers found out she had to miss school for suicidal thoughts with strong urges to overdose.

    I met with Kelsey 10 days after she was released from a hospital to a partial program. Prior to this time, she spent three 3 weeks in the hospital due to intense urges to end her life. After spending 14 days in the hospital and suffering from an allergic reaction to her medication, she tried to escape the day of release by jumping out of the hospital room window. She had to be chemically restrained (i.e., given medication to calm her down) and re-admitted to the hospital for 7 more days. Once subdued, she was able to sleep and rest until 5am the next morning. By 5am she was agitated and angry which resulted in her running down the hospital's hallway screaming "help me! help me! help me!" A nurse was able to calm her down long enough to give her a dose of Valium (i.e., an anti-anxiety medication used for panic attacks). After being released on day 21 from the hospital, she ended up declining again. She tried to poison herself by swallowing bleach at her grandmother's house. Thankfully her father was home that day and smelled the bleach and poured it out before Kelsey could get to it. Because of these behaviors at home, she was sent back to the hospital for immediate treatment over a 24 hour period. Sadly, Kelsey was not eligible for RTF care because she had not shown these behaviors in the past, did not try other forms of treatment before being admitted to the hospital, and responded very well to treatment if given the correct medication. Most mental health professionals strive to keep teens in the "least restrictive environment." This means that mental health professionals would rather a teen visit a hospital for a few days, be released, and sent back home with a referral to a community mental health center or private practice. The goal of psychotherapy in today's world is to keep kids out of an RTF or a program that houses them for long periods of time. This is the result of de-institutionalization, the release of many patients from state psychiatric facilities that occurred in the 1960s. Thankfully Kelsey was able to be stabilized long enough to see me in a partial hospital program.

Partial hospital treatment for suicidal thoughts: Kelsey

I ended up seeing Kelsey for the first time a day after her release from the hospital. Her parents were exhausted and afraid. Kelsey seemed very angry. She was tired of treatment and wanted to move on. She saw no real reason for why she was back in a mental health program. To her, the hospital was enough. This took me some explaining and convincing to do:

Me: Hello Kelsey, my name is Támara and I will be your therapist while you are here. How are you guys?

Amy/Mike: Good, good thank you.

Kelsey: Hi.

Me: Could you tell me a little about why you are here today? I noticed you were hospitalized for 21 days for intense suicidal thoughts and attempts. Is that right?

Kelsey: Yeah, I guess.

Amy: What do you mean you guess? You tried to kill yourself the first time by overdosing on your grandmother's heart medication and cut your wrist. Then the second time you tried to jump out of a hospital window and then later poison yourself with bleach.

Kelsey: Okay mom! Give it a rest already!

Me: Kelsey, I understand your frustration. I would not want to be admitted to a hospital, watched 24/7 by staff, and then end up returning to another program. I'd be angry too. The only reason you are here today is to get you well enough to never have to return to an uncomfortable and scary hospital. Does that make sense?

Kelsey: Yes. But I still don't want to be here.

Me: I get it, I do. How about you tell me what has been bothering you, without your parents in the room, and then we'll bring them back in at the end to complete the intake?

Kelsey: Okay. If I must.

Me: Thank you, Amy and Mike. I will come get you in 30min.

Parents: Okay. Thank you.

Me: Tell me what has been going on at home?

Kelsey: I always felt loved and safe by my parents. They are good parents. The problem is that they are always doing something that doesn't include me.

Me: What do you mean?

Kelsey: They work nonstop and around the clock, even when they are not at work they are on their phones at home or their computers. I try to watch TV shows with them in the evening or do something else like help mom cook but they are always in a rush to get back to work. I think they went crazy when they lost the home.

Me: (Half-smile, look of shock). What do you mean?
Kelsey: They lost the home after my dad lost his job for

getting angry with a customer. He was a manager of a car dealership. My mom had to leave her job 5 months before that because she had to get surgery on her hip. Our home went into foreclosure and we had to move in with my grams (i.e. her short name for grandmother).

Me: Oh. I see. That can be tragic for some kids.

Kelsey: I know! They don't think so though. Then I had to move schools because my grams lives in a totally different county. That made my life a mess. No one likes me. I get bullied. I get teased about being depressed.

Me: I see. Is that what pushed you to consider killing yourself?

Kelsey: Yeah. I lost my home, I lost my hope, I don't have friends, I get bullied almost every single day, and now my parents send me to a hospital. What else is next!?

Me: I totally get that. It sounds as if you are losing more things than you are gaining, especially your freedom. When we feel we have lost the very thing that makes us feel secure we try very hard to regain what we had before. Sometimes what we had will never be again. That means we have to find new meaning and a new level of motivation to move forward. Make sense?

Kelsey: Yes. I hadn't thought of it that way before.

Me: How about we bring your parents back in and complete our intake?

Kelsey: Okay. That's good.

I ended up recommending that Kelsey complete daily group therapy (i.e., an IOP – Intensive Outpatient Program) and weekly individual and family therapy. She was also able to leave her school and start the partial program's school-based program. Her GPA went up and her suicidal thoughts decreased. She ended up seeing me almost everyday in the hallway. She would smile, wave, or greet me with bright eyes. She was stabilizing and doing so much better than before. Kelsey and I eventually discussed returning to her district's school or entering a cyber-based home-schooling program and seeing me part-time for therapy in outpatient therapy. Kelsey and her parents were agreeable to this plan. Because her behaviors stabilized, Kelsey no longer met criteria for a partial program and was being "discharged" to a lower level of care. Kelsey began seeing me for outpatient therapy.

Outpatient therapy for suicidal thoughts: Kelsey

Kelsey began seeing me one time a week for both individual and family therapy. She returned to school to take some classes in-person, while taking other classes at home online. I asked Kelsey if she would sign a consent or authorization for me to coordinate what I know about her with the school counselor. She agreed. I also asked her parents how they felt about this before I called her school. Both parents agreed. I faxed over a copy of the consent to release or obtain information. I confirmed receipt and asked to speak with the school counselor. The school counselor called me back the next day and was able to discuss some of Kelsey's challenges over the past 2 years with me. I offered information about Kelsey's relationship with me and what she is working on. I asked the school counselor if she would email me or call me in the event she notices Kelsey looking sad or depressed. I explained that she is working on developing healthier coping skills such as taking deep breaths, learning about mindfulness and meditation, exercising or engaging in dance, asking for help, and taking a 5-10 minute break. I also mentioned the medication Kelsey was taking so the school nurse would be aware.

Kelsey spent the next year with me in outpatient therapy before leaving the country for one year for a study abroad trip she had earned her senior year of high-school. I completed a discharge form with the family, suggested she speak with her psychiatrist (who had been prescribing her medication), and offered my contact information in the event she would need to call me. Thankfully, Kelsey was able to go off to college without any further challenges with suicidal thoughts or cutting.

Understanding levels of treatment

Kelsey is a prime example of a teen who has severe thoughts of suicide and has made multiple attempts. She struggled for many years with an inability to control her emotions. This led to three different levels of treatment starting with the hospital and ending with outpatient therapy. Kelsey needed a high level of care (but not as high as RTF) to help her control risky and dangerous behaviors. Once these behaviors were under control, Kelsey could consider a lower level of care (i.e., partial hospital program) to help prepare her for an even lower level of care (i.e., outpatient therapy). Because of the intensity of her suicidal thoughts and attempts, Kelsey needed to be in the hospital but she did not qualify for residential treatment because with the right amount of medication and therapy, she was able to function. William was not. William had a chronic history of dangerous behaviors that were exacerbated by oppositional behavior. Kelsey was not oppositional per se. She was depressed, anxious, and suicidal. William struggled with oppositional behaviors including hallucinations (i.e., seeing things that were not present in his environment) and delusions (i.e., having strong beliefs or convictions that something is true when it is not true). He needed 24/7 long-term treatment, while Kelsey needed 24/7 acute or short-term treatment. She was eventually able to attend a partial program (i.e., a program offering education, therapy, and medication) and later an outpatient office. It took William months before he could try a lower level of care such as a partial or outpatient program.

It is very important to remember that mental health treatment is based on a "hierarchical system." This means that services are provided based on the severity of need and the inability to maintain safe behaviors in the community. If a teen is unable to stay in the community, assessment for a higher level of care typically occurs in the hospital after the teen is admitted.

If a teen is a client in an outpatient clinic or private practice, the therapist can assess need and refer you to another mental health professional who can help. This "hierarchical system" is like a ladder and some teens must have experienced a lower level of care (outpatient treatment) before being referred to a higher level (residential programs). When I work with "high risk" teens I typically complete a thorough intake assessment, administer mental health self-report questionnaires, and then recommend treatment services necessary to assist the teen in recovering. In some cases, I end up sending the teen and the parent to the hospital for further assessment and a higher level of care.

Other therapeutic services for suicidal thoughts

Other services that may be available for younger teens (age 14 and younger) would include therapeutic staff support services (i.e., a therapeutic staff worker, trained in behavior management, who can support the teen in coping with his/her environment), a behavior specialist consultant (a professional who works with problematic behaviors), and/or mobile therapists or family based therapists (i.e., therapists who see the client in the home, school, and community). Behavior specialist consultants are also trained in behavior management and can be useful in helping you and your teen apply behavior management skills in all settings. A family based and/or in-home mobile therapist can see your teen at home, in school, and in the community. These mobile therapists provide services similar to an outpatient therapist but only in the home, school, or community and not in an office environment. Some families are offered mobile therapists after a teen leaves residential care, a hospital, or even a partial program. As stated in chapter 3, a "step-down" program (such as partial, family-based, or mobile therapy) helps the teen maintain healthy behaviors outside of the therapeutic relationship which sets them up for success and avoids relapse and/or failure.

Involuntary commitment (302): When a provider hospitalizes a client

A 302 helps a mental health professional ensure the safety and protection of a client, even if that client isn't admitted. A 302 also permits a family member to admit a teen who is engaging in unsafe behaviors. It is the process by which a clinician must weigh and balance the pros and cons of making the decision to commit a client to a hospital. Family members also have to weigh the pros and cons. The process can go terribly wrong if poor decisions are made without forethought. Despite the many reasons for an involuntary commitment, it can be a traumatizing experience including for the therapist. Therapists have a difficult position because they strive to be supportive and caring and yet, must make drastic decisions if a client isn't safe, healthy, or able to care for basic needs. The relationship that seems, to the client, to be a "friendship" can quickly turn in to a relationship with a major power differential. This power differential, once exercised, can cause a client to feel betrayed, hurt, or disappointed. This can then lead a client to drop out of therapy forever.

When it comes to managing suicidal teens, a therapist tends to move from caring, compassionate, and understanding to authoritative and in control of the client's ultimate fate. The changing role of the therapist is what tends to keep client's on guard throughout therapy and possibly even unable to fully trust. A caring therapist tries their hardest to avoid involuntary commitment as it can seriously disrupt the therapeutic relationship and cause scars difficult to heal. You, as the parent, can truly be supportive to your teen by helping them understand the purpose for a 302 and encourage them to be cooperative.

Why 302's are sometimes necessary

As a therapist, involuntary commitment is the last resort for me after hours, days, weeks, or even months of trying to support a high risk teen and ensure their health and safety are maintained. Unfortunately, some mental health professionals (especially those who are inexperienced) may rely on this method to control clients, win a power struggle, or "get rid of" clients who are very difficult and resistant. But this is not what a 302 is.

Involuntary commitment will occur if the following is happening:

- Harm to self or others
- Moderate to extreme self-mutilation
- Threats to harm or kill self or others
- Emotional disturbance and thought disturbance with a history of suicide attempts or gestures
- Impulsivity, suicidal ideation, threats, poor anger management, SIB that is severe (cutting, burning, etc) with the intent of killing self.
- Violence and threats toward others.

Any child under the age of 14 has no say in how mental health treatment should go. They also do not have power over signing themselves into or out of the hospital. You, as the legal guardian or parent, will be held liable for making these decisions. A mental health provider cannot override your wishes. In some cases, a 302 may be initiated without the parent knowing what to expect or how to help. Sadly, many parents go through this experience knowing very little. More challenges often arise with teens who are aware of their "legal right" to make treatment decisions. Some teens make decisions that could negatively impact their safety without the parent's input. In many states, teens age 14 and older (despite being under the legal age of 18) can make treatment decisions such as:

- Stoping or starting medication.
- Starting or ceasing from seeing a therapist.
- Deciding whether they'd like to sign themselves in or out of the hospital.
- Deciding if they'd like their guardian or parent to know what is happening in treatment.

In addition, the 302 process isn't as simple as parents would like it to be because of the power the hospital holds. Hospitals can determine, without the input of the family, if a teen truly needs to be in the hospital or not. In other words, hospitals can determine, based on behaviors exhibited by the teen during the psychiatric evaluation, if hospital care is needed at the time of the evaluation. A teen must be "a danger to self or others" which is a very broad hospital and state policy that can be interpreted in many ways. For example, you may believe that your teen is a danger to himself or others because he tried to electrocute himself after being told to do his homework. A hospital may reject him for treatment if the evaluating clinician or doctor does not believe he will continue to be in imminent danger. *Imminent danger* is often interpreted by hospitals and states to involve suicidal behaviors, self-harming behaviors, or inadequate care that has a high chance of causing significant bodily harm. Some teens with eating disorders who refuse to eat and tend to engage in starving themselves can also be admitted. But again, this will depend on what the hospital says and observes about the teen. If your teen is calm, in control of their emotions, is denying suicidal or homicidal thoughts, and is being cooperative during the psychiatric evaluation, the hospital is likely to discharge your teen with recommendations for further treatment elsewhere.

"Imminent danger" can mean many things to many people, which is why some hospitals often disagree with parents who believe their teen is in imminent danger. To states and hospitals, imminent danger is determined when injury or death is very close to becoming a reality. "Potentially harmful" is not enough for a hospital to admit your teen. This is a sad reality that healthcare providers, advocates, families, and grassroots efforts have battled for years.

If you are interested in learning more about these state laws and ways to help your loved one, you may learn more at www.treatmentadvocacycenter.org.

Voluntary treatment (201) for suicidal thoughts

Your best option is to help your teen consider voluntary commitment into a hospital. Voluntary commitment (or a 201) to a hospital is appropriate for a teen who is willing to be signed into a hospital or agrees to sign themselves into the hospital. The process is often less dramatic and complicated. It also allows you and your teen to have more control over length of stay. Your teen can arrive in the emergency room with you or another adult who can assist with paperwork and providing good details on the reason for admission. You or your teen will sign paperwork that will allow them to receive treatment for a certain length of time, often more time than what is offered in a 302. For example, a 302 admission will last between 48-72 hours to stabilize the teen with the ultimate goal of releasing them sooner than later. A voluntary commitment can last between 48hrs to a little less than one week. But for the most part, you, your teen, and the doctor or clinician will determine the exact length of stay. This approach to obtaining hospital level care is less traumatizing than a 302. A 302 will not only include forcing a teen into the hospital against his or her will, but will also include the police accompanying the teen to the hospital. During a 302 process a therapist may also request police do a "wellness visit" to wherever the teen is to check on them while they complete the paperwork for a 302 petition. This will depend on state law as states across the nation in the U.S. may be different. A 201 allows everyone to relax and remain in control of the next steps. It is less traumatizing, dramatic, and angering.

Referrals and follow-up

If your teen has been in any of the above services for mental health treatment or suicidal thoughts it will be important to ask for a referral if the RTF, hospital, partial program, or outpatient clinic does not offer a referral for further services. A referral is a recommendation for further treatment following the successful completion of a therapeutic program. Referrals from a mental health or medical professional are often helpful for the simple fact that you and your teen would call the referral (i.e., a doctor, therapist, or other mental health professional), ask if new clients are being accepted, and ask to schedule an appointment. The mental health professional who provided the referral information to you may also complete the paperwork necessary for scheduling a first appointment. Depending on the needs of the family, if I am referring a family for further mental health treatment I will often complete the paperwork and get the first appointment scheduled. It is often one of the most beneficial ways to encourage families to follow through as well. In many cases, the referral source (i.e., the person making the recommendation for further treatment) will fax over records to the new treatment provider. In cases where this does not automatically occur, you have the right to request your teen's record be faxed to the new treatment provider. Having records faxed to the new treatment provider ensures that appropriate treatment continues and that the new provider can pick up where the previous treatment ended. If you feel that coordination of care between two treatment providers is unnecessary or harmful to your teen, you can call and ask that the consent be withdrawn. Please check your state laws prior to requesting the consent be withdrawn. Different states will have different laws, standards, and expectations.

Community supports

Community supports for teens can be wonderful, especially when teens begin to feel a sense of community in their heart and soul. For many of my teen clients I encourage them to reach out to their local church or youth group leaders for support, volunteer for a great cause in their neighborhood, or attend a community-based program for youths who come together in a community to meet new people. In the community in which I am teamed up with a group private practice, many of the youths in the neighborhood report feeling more connected to their community when engaging with neighbors and others living or working near them. I find this to be very helpful to teens who cannot make friends in school. Examples of some community events that may be helpful include: exhibits, sporting events, auctions, auto-shows, plays, marathons, films, lectures, dance competitions, art festivals, school functions, volunteer work, etc. If you check your local newspaper you may have a "community calendar" that lists the various community-based programs in your teen's school district or your neighborhood. Such programs are often free and occur during the evening or weekend. Because schools are often more involved in community events than individual families, teachers typically play a major role in encouraging community involvement for teens who are at risk for or who are struggling with suicidal ideation(s). Don't be afraid to ask your teen's teacher for community resources.

Putting it all together

It is important that you and your teen have some idea of what kind of treatment they may need to recover from suicidal thoughts. To get started, you can contact your teen's primary care physician or local crisis support hotline to ask for information on local mental health agencies. A PCP can make a referral to a mental health professional for further care if needed. If teachers are aware of your teen's mental health challenges, they can also be helpful during this process by suggesting a local mental health therapist you can contact or by providing a list of community-based programs in your area. Once you schedule your teen's first appointment, you will need to make a list of questions you and your teen would like to ask a treatment provider. These questions will help you and your teen decide if the therapist is a good fit or has an understanding of the main problem. Asking for a free consultation or meeting to discuss concerns about the teen's symptoms may be helpful. Some providers are eager to meet with parents to discuss potential treatment options for "free." All you have to do is ask if the therapist provides "free" consultations. In the event that your teen is not a good fit with the treatment provider, clinical approach, or level of care, the therapist may refer your teen to a more appropriate treatment provider. If not, you should ask for a referral or suggestion on where to go next for treatment if your teen is not improving. I encourage you to discuss this with your teen first.

NOTES

CHAPTER 6

Safety Planning From A Trauma-informed Perspective

"When little people are overwhelmed by big emotions, it's our job to share our calm, not their chaos."

- L.R. Knost

When I began my career journey shortly after graduate school I had been working in residential treatment facilities (RTF's) providing individual, family, and group counseling to youths between the ages of 9 and 19. The RTF's had trained its workers in a modality known as the Sanctuary Model of Trauma-informed Care. The foundation of this approach to treating traumatized youths is that trauma is pervasive, complex, and bio-psycho-social. This means that there are biological (brain chemicals, genes), psychological (intrapersonal and interpersonal), and social (environmental, nurture, and social learning) that influences the ways in which trauma affects an individual. Trauma affects every aspect of the individual and the only way to change the negative affects of the trauma is to change the "mental models" upon which thought and action are based. In other words, the Sanctuary Model strives to change the way the traumatized child thinks, acts, and relates to other. One may surmise that, in many ways, the Sanctuary Model reflects principles of the Bible such as togetherness and cohesiveness, teamwork and building connectedness, commitment to emotional intelligence and learning ways to manage emotions, commitment to open communication and being open about feelings and thoughts, commitment to social learning and adopting better ways of building cognitive skills such as reasoning, commitment to democracy and ensuring all have the right to be heard, commitment to nonviolence and ensuring that everyone in the environment never feels threatened, commitment to social responsibility.

The idea behind the sanctuary model is to help individuals within organizations (where trauma treatment is being provided) change their environment to a more cohesive, innovative, and creative context within which healing (psychologically, emotionally, socially) can occur. In the two residential facilities I worked in the Sanctuary Model was not only implemented for the youths within the facility but also the adults. Many of the employees including the mental health professionals were required to take the Sanctuary Model trainings every single year. Sadly, despite the frequent trainings and "refresher courses" provided, many of the workers failed to fully understand the model and implement it. Although the theoretical basis for such as model is well understood, the ways in which it is implemented or not implemented can create more trauma. While I am not a die-heart fan of the model, I do believe some principles can be helpful when working with a teen who has experienced trauma. Even more, I see its relevance in working with suicidal youths as well. So I encourage you, as the parent, to try to incorporate some of the above sanctuary principles into your home environment. When teens know everyone in the household is making a commitment to ensure the environment is safe, comfortable, happy, friendly, and peaceful, they often adapt to things much better. For most parents, once they find out that their teen is considering suicide they often jump into "remedy mode" and are ready to make major changes in an attempt to "fix things." This model may serve as a good first step for your family. Instead of opting to change things, it may be more helpful to incorporate certain principles and values into the family routine. For example, I once counseled a 15 year old who had been cutting and attempting suicide since the age of 12. When her adopted parents found out, they implemented a "vacation plan" that included a full summer road trip in an attempt to help their daughter develop motivation for fun things in life. Sadly, this only led to her becoming more suicidal as she was often stuck in the backseat of an SUV with her three younger brothers. A more sound plan would have been for the family to incorporate, one at a time, activities that the family can test out. If you want to incorporate some of the Sanctuary Model principles into your family routine giving your teen a chance to express themselves and be heard (commitment to democracy), ask questions or talk to you (open communication), and express their opposing views in a peaceful fashion (commitment to nonviolence), can make a hug impact.

The Sanctuary Model is an evidence-based, trauma-informed system focused on organizational change. It encourages individuals to commit themselves to being better human beings with moral standards from which to work from when encountering a trauma survivor. The S.E.L.F. Model (an extension of the Sanctuary Model) is a tool I previously used in individual, family, and group therapy with teens suffering from post traumatic stress disorder (PTSD). The "Sanctuary Toolkit" includes a variety of tools for addressing traumatic stress. One of the most useful (and less complicated) tools for many of my suicidal teen clients is the SELF-Model. Although it has not been researched specifically with suicidal teens, it has been a tool useful for me to stimulate difficult conversations about thoughts and feelings. It is a psychoeducational framework that provides some insight into the road of healing and recovery from traumatic experiences.

SELF is an acronym for Safety, Emotions, Loss, and Future:

- **Safety** - teaches teens to focus on learning about and fostering psychological, social, emotional, and physical safety. The idea is that the first step toward recovery is attaining a sense of safety and continuing to feel safe in all domains of one's life.

- **Emotions** - Teens who have been traumatized struggle with emotion dysregulation. In order to heal and develop appropriate management of emotions, teens must learn to gain control of their emotions. An example of this would be coping skills or the safety plan (which we will discuss later in this chapter).

- **Loss** - Teens must learn to let go of the things that traumatized them in order to grow and change and embrace the positives that the future may behold for them.

- **Future** - Teens must learn to focus on the here-and-now and let go of the past. Focusing on the future and staying grounded in newly developed skills for managing traumatic stress is important. One way to do this is by journaling, praying, spending time alone, and learning about mindfulness meditation.

There is a "hook" on the sanctuaryweb.com page about the SELF-Model that says:

> "When things get tough, I put SELF first. There is no compromising my SELF worth. It's the only thing that helps when the SELF hurts...."

It is often helpful when families "create a sancturary" for the suicidal teen within the home. Home should be a place of comfort, a place of restoration, and a place of peace.

According to Dr. Sandra Bloom, MD (Psychiatrist and proponent of the Sanctuary Model):

> "...Creating sanctuary' refers to the shared experience of creating and maintaining physical, psychological, social, and moral safety within a social environment (any social environment) and thus reducing systemic violence and counteracting the destructive parallel processes that are a result of chronic and unrelenting stress in a vulnerable species."

My use of the SELF-Model with a suicidal teen with a traumatic past

Melanie was a 13-year-old biracial female who had experienced multiple incidents of sexual abuse from her paternal uncle for 5-years before her grandmother found out. When her grandmother died she was placed in foster care for the next 3-years before being adopted by a wealthy family in California. Once adopted, she began to struggle with symptoms of depression which included isolation/withdrawal, depressed mood, irritability, self-injurious behaviors (i.e., cutting, burning herself), and suicidal ideation. She attempted suicide on 3 occasions which included overdose, hanging, and cutting her wrist. She was unsuccessful with each attempt, but very eager to try it again once she had the opportunity. Her adoptive parents brought her to me shortly after her 13th birthday when they found her hanging an iron bar from her bedroom closet. Melanie presented to the intake with an irritable mood and affect. She was emotionally detached from everyone and refused to answer questions about her suicide attempts. Her parents did most of the talking which angered Melanie. I asked both parents to take a passive approach in an attempt to get Melanie to speak up. It worked. Melanie began to explain the reason for her suicide attempts which include emotion dysregulation when angered by something she heard or saw, thinking about the things she has lost over the course of her childhood, and feeling unsafe because of perceived threats within her environment. I decided to use the SELF-Model as a way to encourage Melanie to process her emotions about the trauma she had previously experienced. I began the exploration of her trauma once her parents left the room.

Therapist: Melanie, could I engage you in an activity focused on exploring some of your trauma history? I know we haven't really talked about your past trauma and that you may be slightly reluctant. But I do think it might help for me to demonstrate what therapy might look like for you.

Melanie: Sure. Why not.

Therapist: Great. Thank you. Please write the word SELF down the side of your paper in perpendicular fashion. Then write the words "Safety, Emotions, Loss, and Future" sideways.

Melanie: Ok. Now what?

Therapist: Let's explore the first part which is safety. Now that you have been adopted by a wonderful family you have most likely thought about your past trauma. Sometimes when we feel safe and loved we begin to explore and process the negative things that have happened to us. It's as if the safe environment encourages us to re-work things in our mind and heart. Have you gone through this process in your mind and heart yet?

Melanie: Yes. I used to think a lot about my real mom and why she gave me to my grandmother. My grandmother was 67 when my mom left me with her.

She was so cruel because she asked my grandmother to babysit me and then never came back for me. My grandmother realized that this was my mom's way of saying she didn't want me. My uncle would come over my grandmother's house and spend a lot of time with me. He would play games with me, take me out for ice cream, take me to the movies, take me shopping, and anything else I really wanted to do. He was an awesome uncle!

Therapist: I see. It sounds as if your uncle was doing something child molesters do which is known as "grooming." Have you ever heard of this term?

Melanie: No. What does it mean?

Therapist: Basically it is the idea that the adult attempts to gain respect and trust from a child in order to manipulate them and get what they ultimately want. It is a common tactic of predators. Taking you everywhere and getting you everything you wanted helped him to become a "treasure" in your mind which led to trust and bonding. This trust and bonding would later become the very tool he would use against you. Am I right?

Melanie: Yes. Yes, you are. My grandmother said something like this before.

Therapist: Is this the time you began to have suicidal thoughts?

Melanie:: Yeah. I didn't want to live. I trusted him. Then my grandmother died and I was put in foster care. I tried to kill myself then too.

Therapist:: I see. Life was really coming down on you at this time. And you were so young too.

Melanie:: Yeah. I guess.

Therapist: Can you identify any threats to your physical, emotional, psychological, moral, or social safety when you lived with your grandmother?

Melanie:: Yes. My uncle was a safety threat all the way around. I also felt psychologically unsafe because my grandmother didn't understand I was depressed and struggling. Then I felt emotionally unsafe because no one understood what I was feeling and why. My grandmother thought I was even lying to get out of school. I wasn't!

Therapist:: I see. Very good Melanie. You're doing well. Anything else you can see as far as a threat to your safety?

Melanie:: I can see where I was physically unsafe because my uncle sexually abused me. He didn't even seem to care. He really hurt me.

Therapist: Yes, he did. You most likely felt socially unsafe as well because you didn't trust other people after that. I'm not even sure you actually trust your adoptive parents.

Melanie: I don't know. Maye.

Therapist: Yeah. I think it's a strong possibility. Can you identify any emotions you had during that time?

Melanie: Yes. All of them. I was mad, sad, hopeless, angry, confused, and all the other bad emotions there are. I felt all of them.

Therapist: Yes. I can imagine. What about loss? Can you identify anything you may have lost that meant a lot to you?

Melanie: Well... my biological parents didn't want me. Then my favorite uncle hurt me. Then my grandmother died. Then I was taken out of the family and put into foster care. I lost a lot of my friends too because I had to go to another school. It was really hard for me.

Therapist: I can see how. You had to deal with a lot of change, transition, and emotional instability. Your world was upside down for a bit there. Do you still feel this way?

Melanie: Yeah, sometimes. That's why I start thinking about killing myself. I don't want to go back.

Therapist: I don't blame you at all. I want to teach you a few skills that may help you cope a bit better. I encourage you to maintain an open mind because some of the tools I will teach you will require practice. You may also struggle at times, but that's okay. We all do. We will also discuss problem-solving, making good decisions, staying safe with a safety plan, developing skills to engage in open communication, stress management, and self-soothing, and using coping skills to stay grounded. Does this sound like a plan to you?

Melanie: Yeah. I'm ready I think.

Therapist: That's great to hear! Before we end our intake session can you identify any thing you'd like to focus on for a better future?

Melanie: I don't know if I understand.

Therapist: The SELF-Model focuses on safety, emotions, loss, and future. Future focuses on helping you see what is to come and helping you envision a better future for yourself. Can you think of anything you'd like to see happen in your future?

Melanie: Yeah. I'd like to graduate high-school, find a boyfriend who really cares, go to college, and get a really good job. My grandmother would always tell me I would be a good nurse. Smile.

Therapist: That's awesome! My mom was a nurse for years and she loved working with the geriatric population. Do you know what type of population you would be interested in?

Melanie: I think I would like to be a nurse in an agency for adopted kids. I really wish I had a staff member I could bond with but I didn't. They were all kind of mean.

As you can see through this example, Melanie was able to explore not only areas of her life where she felt unsafe, but the emotions she had in response to feeling unsafe, the loss she experienced, and the future she was hoping to embark upon. The SELF-Model allows me to organize the discussion, keep my client focused on the reason for therapy, and re-focus attention on the future. Melanie and I discussed the true reason for her suicidal thoughts and attempts. She also had the opportunity to pause and reflect on her trauma and its direct influence on her desire to end her life.

As a parent, you can use this same approach when having a discussion with your teen. I like to use this model to build insight and refocus attention on the ultimate goal which is recovering, healing, and growing for the future.

SELF-Model exercise

The SELF-Model can be useful in helping parents and teachers help teens organize what they are feeling and why. Use the SELF-Model exercise below to start the exploration process. This might also be "data" that your teen's therapist or even teacher can use when needed. You can either use pencil to write down responses or re-create it on a blank piece of paper. This activity will give you practice before you introduce this activity to your teen.

Source: Sandra Bloom, MD - sanctuaryweb.com or thesanctuaryinstitute.org.

Safety:

For this model, there are 5 kinds of safety. Use the space below to write down the safety violations you notice for each sub-category (i.e., physical, emotional, psychological, social, & moral).

Physical_____

_____
_____
_____
_____
_____
_____

Emotional_____

_____
_____
_____
_____
_____
_____

Psychological_____

_____
_____
_____
_____

_____

Social_____

_____
_____
_____
_____
_____

Moral_____

_____
_____
_____
_____

Emotions:

Identify emotions that you my have felt or expressed and write them on the line below.

_____
_____
_____
_____

_____

_____

_____

_____

Loss:

Identify the loss that may be contributing to your feelings and write them below.

_____

_____

_____

_____

_____

_____

_____

Future

Identify anything that you feel you could gain out of life despite the trauma. Identify things you would like to learn or do. Write them below.

_____

_____

_____

_____

_____

_____

_____

_____

Trauma-Focused Cognitive Behavior Therapy (TF-CBT)

Trauma-Focused CBT is another model (developed by doctors Tony Mannarino, PhD., Judith A Cohen, MD and Esther Deblinger, PhD.) which focuses on taking steps in a chronological order to treat trauma. Each stage of the model builds upon the other and provides structure to the client. It is a newly developed empirical treatment for children, teens, and families who are trying to heal from a traumatic experience. This approach to treating teens is based on:

- Working with children who have experienced trauma
- Effectiveness with children of diverse backgrounds
- Psychoeducation about the impact of trauma

- Helping parents to develop skills to optimize the child's emotional, psychological, and behavioral adjustment following the trauma.
- Teaching parents co-regulation and helping their child regulate their emotional expression.
- Teaching cognitive coping and teaching the relationship between thoughts, feelings, and behaviors (which I will discuss further in this chapter).
- Developing the trauma narrative which is the story of the traumatic event.
- Healing the child even if the parent, guardian, or caregiver is unavailable.
- Working with children in foster care settings.
- Providing care to youths from a variety of countries which includes various languages.
- Engaging the child in in vivo desensitization and guided imagery to help child face anxiety-provoking memories or events.
- Addressing intrusive symptoms or upsetting memories, avoidance, emotional numbing, and hyper-arousal and mood dysregulation.

- Twelve treatment sessions which include the parent and some kind of "family therapy"
- Is used (and has been used successfully) in home, schools, clinics, residential treatment facilities, and other inpatient settings.

I encourage you to search for a therapist who uses this framewok to treat clients. It can be very helpful to suicidal teens who have a traumatic past. You can locate therapists who treat trauma using TF-CBT by going to http://tfcbt.org.

Activities from TF-CBT that I have used in therapy with suicidal teens

There are many aspects of TF-CBT that I appreciate when working with teens and their parents. TF-CBT provides a concrete foundation upon which to build resilience, awareness, and skills. It is often very concrete and practical for parents and teens to learn from. I really like that "Your Very Own TF-CBT Workbook" is provided by tfcbt.org. You can find the free workbook in both Spanish and English from https://tfcbt.org/tf-cbt-workbook/. Because the manual is easy, practical, and helpful to clients between the ages of 3 and 17 years old,

I often encourage parents to look through the workbook and help their teen(s) complete some of the activities for "homework" outside of therapy. This provides something for my client and I to discuss and build on during subsequent sessions. It also provides some direction for future sessions. It can also encourage both you and your teen to engage in an exploration of the trauma outside of therapy. TF-CBT focuses on conjoint parent-child sessions in which the therapist reveals some of the trauma work that has been done to the parent and engages in connecting the parent to the teen. This phase is regarded as the integration and consolidation phase.

When I meet with families for trauma-informed therapy, I often explain that the goal is to encourage introspection, insight building, and independence. I love teaching teens how to develop the skills and knowledge needed for recovery. I'm of the firm belief that knowledge, primarily self-knowledge (i.e., the knowledge developed on one's own time), is very powerful for facilitating the development of independence. The first activity I love using with teens and their parents is the *safety and crisis plan.*

Safety planning

For most people, safety plan and crisis plan are words used interchangeably to mean the same thing. For me, I use these terms to refer to different concepts. Safety planning is the process by which the teen, parent, and I explore various ways the teen can engage in cognitive coping. A safety plan is a set of skills or tools that will be used by the teen if and when they begin to feel "unsafe" or begin to experience a negative emotion that can result in a crisis. A safety plan is a wonderful way to help teens remember to use their newly developed skills to avert a crisis. Every safety plan is different and is often highly individualized so that it will be effective. For example, a safety plan for a suicidal teen may include a 1-800 number to a suicide hotline, while a safety plan for an oppositional and angry teen may include a short walk to get away. A safety plan is a great way to engage teens in learning how to control their emotions and reactions to emotionally stimulating experiences. A safety plan is typically developed in therapy with a therapist who is capable of helping the teen explore things they can do to avert a crisis. However, safety plans can also be developed by teachers and parents for the home, school, and community.

Development of the safety plan

Below you will find an example of a safety plan that I tend to use with suicidal teens. It focuses on the presenting complaint or problem (i.e., suicidal thoughts, emotional outbursts, irritability, etc), triggers (i.e., someone yelling, someone slamming a door, getting a bad grade, being bullied, etc), warning signs (i.e., increased heart-rate, depressed mood, avoidance, withdrawal or isolation, etc), things that others can do to help them (i.e., pray, talk in a calming tone of voice, call a loved one, use humor, take a walk with them, etc), things that others do that don't seem to help (i.e., reminding them of the rules, yelling or being confrontational, rolling eyes, etc.), and coping skills they are willing to try (i.e., deep breathing, drawing or coloring, calling mom or dad, singing, taking a time out in a quiet space, listening to music, eating something healthy, etc). A safety plan should spell out the teen's needs, limitations, and coping skills. I like to encourage teens to come up with skills that can be used in more than one environment such as in school, at home, or in the community. For example, coping skills that can be used at home and in school is deep breathing or asking for a 5-10 minute break. A coping skill that can be used in the community may include calling mom or dad to talk or listening to music. It is important that teens have coping skills they can adapt to any environment they may be in. I like to quote the teen's complaint or challenge in the safety plan (as you will see below) and then list all of the triggers and warning signs that the teen is struggling. Then list the things others can do to help the teen feel better and gain emotional control. You and the teen will want to sign and date it with the goal of re-visiting the safety plan in the future.

When I see teens for therapy I often update their safety plan every 90 days/3 months to add new things or adjust some of the old things. Some teens grow so fast that the coping skills that once worked may no longer work 90 days from the date of the first safety plan.

Blank example safety plan

Complaint or challenge: "Getting angry really fast"

<u>**Triggers/Things that make me worse:**</u>

1._____
2._____
3._____
4._____
5._____
6._____

Warning signs: Things that indicate a crisis is likely to occur

1. _____
2. _____
3. _____
4. _____
5. _____
6. _____

Coping skills: Things that can help you cope better

1. _____
2. _____
3. _____
4. _____
5. _____
6. _____
7. _____

Things that others can do to help:

1. _____
2. _____
3. _____
4. _____

5._____

6_____

Parent signature (if applicable)_____

Date:_____

Therapist signature (if applicable)_____

Date:_____

Teen Signature_____

Date:_____

This safety plan can be shown to the teen's teacher and/or therapist as it provides great information and details on what triggers and helps calm your teen.

Example of the safety plan I used with Melanie

Complaint or challenge: "Feeling suicidal when thinking about my trauma"

Triggers/Things that make me worse:

1. Being reminded of the rules while being yelled at

2. Feeling unsafe and all alone. Withdrawing and isolating.
3. Being reminded of the trauma if someone mentions it on a bad day

Warning signs:
Increased heart rate and heart palpitations
Crying and tearfulness for no reason
Being irritable and easily angered with family and friends
Skipping school and refusing to get up in the morning
Sleeping all the time and staying in room for long periods of time

Coping skills:
1. Talking to my therapist
2. Drawing or coloring
3. Taking deep breaths
4. Taking a very long walk with dog
5. Talking to my parents or teacher
6. Listening to music
7. Asking to take a break for 5-10 min
8. Looking at my picture book of fun memories
9. Closing my eyes and imagining my "safe place"

Things that others can do to help:
1. Remind me of my coping skills
2. Let me take a walk or break
3. Draw or color with me
4. Give me a hug
5. Remind me of something positive or fun coming up in the future like my birthday or a vacation

Parent signature (if applicable)
Billy Aweday   Date: 9/15/2015

Therapist signature (if applicable)
Támara Hill, MS, NCC, CCTP, LPC Date: 9/15/2015

Teen Signature
Melanie Aweday   Date: 9/15/2015

Crisis planning

As stated above, crisis planning is the process of identifying ways to manage the crisis and prevent any emotional, psychological, or environmental damage that may occur. For example, Melanie reported feeling suicidal on multiple occasions and attempting suicide during moments when she felt hopeless and isolated. She had a safety plan completed which was laminated for her to carry around in her wallet or pockets. However, there were times she abandoned her safety plan and felt it wouldn't help her manage her emotions. She completely ignored any suggestions or promptings from the adults around her to use a coping skill listed on her safety plan. Once she felt completely escalated and out of control, it was too late to engage in using coping skills. I was then challenged to help she and her adoptive mother consider ways to manage a crisis.

Crisis planning, for me, is the process of looking at multiple ways to manage emotional escalation and return everyone, including the teen, back to baseline (i.e., a state of calm and control). A crisis happens when emotion regulation fails. Coping skills are used to prevent a crisis. But in some cases, a safety plan or coping skills aren't enough to stop a crisis from happening. As a result, it is important that you and your teen (along with the therapist and/or teacher) identify ways to manage a crisis. Every crisis plan is different and I'm sure, with a quick Google search, you would find multiple approaches to developing a crisis plan. But when I develop a crisis plan with parents and teens I often focus on psychological, behavioral, and emotional preparation.

Psychological preparation

Psychological preparation includes ensuring that you have a plan beforehand. Write down, in a notebook, things you could do if an emergency occurs. For example, if your teen begins to hallucinate or express delusional beliefs, write down what your first step will be. Will you stop responding to your teen? Will you avoid conflict at all cost? Will you take a more passive approach? Will you validate your teen's thoughts and feelings but avoid agreeing with them? Will you call your teen's therapist or psychiatrist? Will you encourage hospitalization? Psychological preparation also includes self-care before the crisis. You have to help yourself before you can help your teen. Are you eating right? Sleeping right? Or exercising? Would you be ready for a crisis if you needed to be? It also involves reminding yourself that a crisis will happen. You want to make sure that you are realistic about the fact that a crisis will happen at some point and that you will have to be ready for whatever that entails. Are you ready?

Behavioral preparation

Behavioral preparation includes focusing on things you *can* do such as:

- Knowing whom you will call or contact before the crisis
- Knowing how you will subdue threatening behaviors (i.e., by walking away, calling the police, leaving the house, locking yourself in a bedroom, etc).
- Knowing what you will do (i.e., reminding your teen that you love them, initiating a hug, etc.).

Emotional preparation

Emotional preparation includes being mindful of how you will be affected emotionally by the crisis and coming up with ways to cope better. We cannot predict how we will act during or after the crisis but we can have a plan in place for coping with emotions. It is important that you prepare by:

- Thinking about who you will or could talk to following the crisis
- Considering if therapy would benefit you in learning new ways to cope
- Exploring your emotions through journaling or mindfulness-based activities such as meditation or guided imagery.
- Exploring if medication for anxiety or depression might benefit you
- Considering marital or family therapy to learn skills or discuss challenges

Preparing for a crisis can help you feel less vulnerable when a crisis occurs. Keep in mind that there will be a situation you will not be prepared for. Don't beat yourself up! Developing and implementing the crisis plan requires practice. When I worked in residential treatment facilities it took me almost 2-3 years before I felt comfortable navigating a crisis and implementing the treatment plan. Thankfully, I have only been apart of two separate physical restraints involving a 10-year-old boy from the U.S. and a 9-year-old girl from Kenya. Both restraints were traumatizing to not only myself but the kids. As a result, I often encourage parents (and teachers) to debrief with the teen and family following a crisis situation. Debriefing is the process of discussing what happened and why shortly after the crisis (and once everyone calms down). You can discuss reasons in the future for having to resort to using the crisis plan again. Below is an example of a debriefing I did with William (from chapter 5) when he engaged in physical violence toward staff in the residential treatment facility he was admitted to.

Debriefing example with William from RTF

Therapist: William, what happened out there? What led up to this physical restraint from staff?

William: I DON'T KNOW AND I DON'T WANT TO TALK ABOUT IT...OK.

Therapist: I understand William. Would you please not yell at me. I'm only here to figure out what happened, how I can help, and if I need to discuss better ways of helping you with staff. Are you calm enough to talk to me or should I come back later?

William: Yeah. I guess.

Therapist: Ok. Thank you. What happened, from your perspective, that led up to staff restraining you?

William: I was playing with a toy my mom brought here for me and they told me I couldn't have it because they didn't approve of it yet. I got mad and slammed my door. I then put my bed up against the door and tried to hang myself. I didn't want to lose my percentage points. I worked too hard for them.

Therapist: Sigh. Oh boy William. Remember you and I talked about taking drastic measures and what can happen if you don't cooperate at times?

William: Yes. But I really wanted this toy because my mom gave it to me. I barely get to see her and she bought me the one thing I wanted for my birthday and they want to take it from me.

Therapist: I understand. I do. But that's what I'm here for William. You have to cooperate with staff, talk to me about it if you need to, and wait on me to help you figure out a way to get your toy back. Isn't that better than getting restrained?

William: Yes. But you weren't here!

Therapist: Remember what I told you when you first came here William about learning to wait? You really couldn't play with your toy anyway because it was time for bed and staff makes all of you put your things away for bedtime.

William: I guess.

Therapist: It was a power struggle that you didn't need to engage in William. Did they tell you what the consequences were for leading everyone into a restraint with you?

William: No. They just said they would talk to you.

Therapist: Ok. Well, you will most likely lose TV time and snacks until you are able to get your reward points back up to 90%. You are listed on the wall as having 50% points right now. If you follow the rules, avoid restraints, and do as you are told William you should be fine by Friday.

William: Ok. I can do that.

Therapist: I believe you can too. Let me talk to staff about what we discussed and we'll keep moving forward from there.

William: Ok Ms. Támara. Thank you.

Therapist: You're welcome my dear. I'll talk to you later this week during our session.

As you can see in this example, I debriefed with William and had him explain what happened. I also explained what the consequences would be for his behavior. You and your teen's teachers can do this as well in the event you find something out or need to address the teen about suicide. Parents do this all the time without realizing it. You find something out, you and your teen get angry, and then your teen walks off angry and slams the door. You knock 2 hours later and talk to them about the entire event. This is the same approach with debriefing. It is important to be patient, compassionate, and yet firm during the debriefing process. You want to express your displeasure with the behavior but also display patience and compassion. You want to express that you understand why the event happened but that you do not want the event to happen again. In many cases, debriefing can contribute to building a bond and increasing trust. Teens who are suicidal and struggling with a traumatic past already feel they cannot trust others. Debriefing provides the opportunity for you (and even your teen's teacher) to build rapport and trust. Think of debriefing as a way to revisit the crisis, process and explore it, and then finalize it with a plan for better behavior or ways to cope in the future.

Putting it all together

Most teens who have a traumatic past are very likely to struggle with suicidal thoughts, gestures, and attempts. When this happens it can be useful to explore what is triggering the suicidal thoughts and gestures. Exploring the trauma history will be an important first step. Trained mental health professionals should engage teens in exploring their trauma history. You or your teen's teacher can also help by suggesting journaling of thoughts and feelings or talking to the teen's therapist about their thoughts and feelings. Teens who struggle with suicidal thoughts should have a safety plan. You or the teen's teacher can develop the safety plan. The safety plan should include multiple ways the teen can de-escalate and control their emotions. A crisis plan can be developed as well.

The best way to help teens avert a crisis is to help them identify ways to cope and rely on their support system for help. If a crisis does happen, as it will at times, teens and parents need tools to help them make the appropriate decisions to de-escalate the crisis. Once families de-escalate the crisis, they should debrief and review the crisis with the teen. Reviewing the crisis with the teen isn't bringing things back up to cause turmoil. It is the process of exploring and processing what happened, why it happened, and how to make things better in the future. Resistant and oppositional teens may not like this process but I encourage you to discuss the crisis in some capacity shortly after the event. I don't particularly like debriefing to occur hours or days later because learning may not occur once the teen begins to forget the emotions, thoughts, and behaviors associated with the crisis. Debriefing can be done by you, the parent, or a teacher. Some parents prefer to take notes while talking with their teen about a crisis that happened. Taking notes provides a way to track the date and time of the crisis so that patterns can be found.

For further information on the impact of trauma on the psycho-bio-social development of children and teens, visit my blog: http://blogs.psychcentral.com/caregivers or my website: http://www.anchoredinknowledge.com and search for the word "trauma" in the search engine.

NOTES

CHAPTER 7

Maintaining Treatment Services

And

Staying Organized

"Be who you needed when you were young."

- author unknown

Much of what therapists do is ensure their clients are supported in everything that they do. If your teen is blessed and fortunate enough to have a good therapist, you are probably well aware of what this support looks like. Emails, follow-up calls, faxes, copies, suggested books or articles, recommendations, and referrals all come from good therapists. But so does the development of healthy emotional bonds. The job of a therapist can easily mirror that of a parent, especially when the client is a teen. It has been my experience that many of my teen clients become bonded to me in such a way that the bond itself was therapeutic. My voice becomes therapeutic, my words hold a different power, and sometimes appropriate touch (i.e., hugs, a hand-shake, pat on the arm, high-five, etc) becomes reinforcing. For the parent (and sometimes the teacher involved), the therapeutic bond, the skill of the therapist, and the support displayed by the therapist are all greatly appreciated during the mental health journey. It is these things that not only keeps parents breathing a sigh of relief, but also the teen. In my experience, the one most feared thing for teens is not knowing who they will be talking to.

The therapeutic bond

Maintaining treatment services involves so much more than attending sessions every week, completing paperwork such as treatment plans, and maintaining your insurance. While these things are very important for continuity of care, one of the most powerful determinants of continuing mental health treatment is the therapeutic alliance. Without the therapeutic bond, therapy would be a chore, an activity only engaged in to achieve a goal (i.e., reduce suicidal thoughts, increase compliance, promote emotional stability, etc.). The therapeutic bond is what binds everyone (i.e., the parent, the teen, and the therapist) together for a set period of time so that the ultimate goal of therapy may be achieved. Included below is an email from a parent who had brought her daughter to see me for therapy for a little over a year. When she and her daughter felt ready to venture out on their own without therapy, her mother sent me an email that I will never, ever forget. Her email was a testament to our therapeutic bond:

> "Hi, Kelsey asked me to text you to let you know that she would like to stop coming to her appointments at this time. She is doing so much better and she seems to be happy and adjusting well to life. But please if you switch cell numbers please keep us posted on that!! And please know at first sign of any trouble I will be contacting you!!! You have done so much for our Kelsey and I truly appreciate it!!! You have become a part of our family and we wish nothing but the best for you!!!"

After I wiped a few tears and steadied myself I replied:

> "Hi Missy, Thanks for letting me know. That is wonderful and I'm glad to hear that. That's what therapy is all about, helping you guys get to a place where you feel good enough to stop coming to therapy. If you need anything please let me know, feel free to send a text, and email or stop by. You know where I am so if you need anything I'm here to help. Take good care and all the best to you!"

Her mother decided to send one last heartfelt thank you:

> "Thank you so much. I can't even put into words how much you have helped us/Kelsey. You have changed our lives for the better!!!!"

I was absolutely flabbergasted by the humble words of a loving mother to a therapist who grew to really care about her client (i.e., her daughter). My client was an amazing young lady, full of promise but unable to see it herself. She and her family were wonderful clients. Her mother and father's gratitude is a prime example of a parent who maintained treatment services based on the bond between the therapist and client. She didn't maintain treatment services based on dedication she felt she owed to her insurance company or because she felt if she were to drop out I would misjudge her. She maintained treatment services because she felt her daughter was benefiting. She felt her daughter was learning, growing, and changing for the better.

Maintaining open communication with your teen and the therapist

Some parents go through a lot trying to stay involved in the treatment of their teens. Teens are often looking for ways to exhibit their new-found independence and privacy. The last thing an adolescent wants is to have to tell mom and dad everything that was discussed in therapy. I am of the firm belief that teens need a certain level of privacy in order to flourish and figure out who they are apart from their parents. Teens also deserve privacy when it comes to mental health treatment because there are certain topics teens just don't feel comfortable sharing with their parents. Most of the parents I have worked with over the years are very understanding of this. Unfortunately, some parents are not.

Can you remember how you were as a teen? Despite the fact that I was completely conjoined with my mother's hip throughout my adolescence, I needed my fair share of privacy and independence. My mother allowed me to have privacy and independence because she had no reason to take it away. If your teen has been dishonest or has hidden things from you in the past, they need to know that they will have to work on building that trust back so they can enjoy their natural desire for privacy. That also goes for therapy as well. If your teen has a history of blowing things out of proportion, exaggerating details, or lying, it may be helpful to have some one-on-one conversations with your teen's therapist either in person or by email. I would tell your teen that you will not disclose information that could be damaging to the relationship. I would explain that you want to ensure they are getting the best mental health care and part of ensuring that is sharing some details with their therapist. If this poses a problem, perhaps you and your teen can meet with the therapist together and then your teen can "review" the email or text to the therapist before you send it. Or you and your teen can schedule 15-20 minute "check-ins" with the therapist. Whatever you decide is best for your family, your teen's therapist should hear from you every now and then. Your teen should always know when you have made contact with their therapist. A major part of helping teens maintain mental health services is ensuring they feel safe. Teens need to know they can trust the adult (i.e., the therapist) to support them at all times. The therapeutic alliance is built when a teen feels they can freely talk or share information without the parent finding out about it. When I work with teens who would like their parents to drop them off, stay in the waiting area, stay in the car, or be completely uninvolved, I often ask the teen if I could share certain details that need to be shared such as having frequent suicidal thoughts, engaging in unprotected sex, mixing alcohol and drugs, mixing alcohol and prescription drugs, driving without a license, hiding dating violence, etc. If you think this approach would really be helpful to your teen you may want to suggest this approach to your teen's therapist.

Some teens may also be open to the idea of using virtual therapy to include the parent(s). For example, my Highmark insurance clients will often meet with me in-person for more serious sessions and then "check-in" with me virtually for less serious sessions. I have used HIPAA-Compliant virtual therapy programs for sessions that will include me catching up with the parent. The teen is also apart of this session. This approach helps the teen feel they are still somewhat in control of what is happening with their treatment and allows the parent some time to ask questions and connect with the therapist. It may be helpful to you, as the parent, to go to the session prepared but not overly prepared. You don't want to have all of your articles, notes, etc. lined up because this may trigger your teen to feel anxious or even like they are in trouble. You don't want them to dread the meeting. You just want to have some well thought out questions ready to ask. If your teen has a really good therapist, the therapist will lead the session and be open to answering your questions. I encourage conversation with your teen about the session before it happens. Ask them what they are hoping you say or not say. Ask them what they would rather you not talk about. Once you know, you can weigh whether you should oblige them or not.

Obtaining consent and knowing how to make contact with the therapist

In order to be able to speak with your teen's therapist, you should always have consent. Even if your therapist doesn't mention it, you can ask to sign a consent so that you can share and release information if needed. This relevant for teens who are 14 years old and older. Any child under the age of 14 automatically loses the right to conceal information. They are not afforded the same amount of privacy and confidentiality as a 14 year old would be. Consent allows you to contact the therapist without having to obtain permission from your teen each time you feel important information needs to be shared. If your teen refuses to give you consent to speak with the therapist, the therapist may "break confidentiality" (which is our legal and moral right) if you need to know information that is life threatening to your teen. Of course, this depends largely on the personal and professional style and ethics of the therapist. Otherwise, you may not hear from your teen's therapist at all.

If you find that you are concerned about certain things such as your daughter dating a drug abuser, your son selling heroin, your teen getting high or drunk on school property, etc. you should contact the therapist in some fashion to alert them to the threatening behavior you have witnessed or been told about. You can do this by sending the therapist an email (or voicemail) and preface it by stating something similar to "I wanted to make you aware of some important information and do not expect a reply due to privacy and confidentiality...." It will be important to respect the professional position of your teen's therapist by only contacting the therapist (you do not have consent to contact in the first place) when necessary. I have heard horror stories of some therapists being stalked, harassed, and followed by parents who have absolutely no legal right to interfere with therapy. The therapist does not have to respond to you if there isn't a consent signed by a teen 14 years old or older. This is important to respect and keep in mind.

It is also important to keep in mind that state laws such as **HIPAA** (Health Insurance Portability & Accountability Act of 1996) grants teens the right to their privacy. However, I do encourage you to reach out to the therapist if your teen is in danger, their health is declining, or something else serious occurs. Other than that, teens should have privacy. In some ways you may feel reaching out to your teen's therapist (without your teen's awareness) is going behind their back which can cause rifts in the parent-child relationship. But you must keep in mind that you will only take these steps if, and only if, you feel your teen's safety is being jeopardized. If you do decide to contact your teen's therapist without their permission I think it would be okay to inform your teen about it. Explain your reasoning and why you felt the therapist needed the information. Explain that you will only contact their therapist if you feel there is a real need to do it. Make it clear that you do not have a problem with contacting your teen's therapist with them being present. Try to be as transparent, authentic, and calm as possible.

Maintaining open communication with a therapist through virtual sessions or face-time

Some therapists are willing to do whatever it takes to ensure parents stay connected with them throughout the therapeutic process with the teen. Your teen's therapist may be open to virtual family sessions focused on keeping you updated and informed. Virtual sessions will depend on a few factors such as state laws, ethics codes, professional style of the therapist, your teen's therapeutic needs, and insurance. I encourage you to talk to your teen's therapist about the possibility of incorporating virtual sessions. Virtual sessions can possibly consist of you or your teen catching up on progress or lack of progress, setting and reviewing treatment goals, discussing a minor incident, creating a crisis plan, or something similar. Although sensitive matters should really occur in the office environment with the therapist present, some therapists have had advanced training in how to broach sensitive topics during virtual sessions. Sometimes weather, family travel, and other events can prevent a teen from always being present in a therapist's office. Teens who are being raised in rural areas, in military families, or in remote areas can greatly benefit from virtual sessions. And virtual sessions may be extremely beneficial for teens who struggle with severe social anxiety, medical conditions, or getting out of the house on time. Whatever the reason for virtual sessions may be, keep in mind that your teen's therapist may be willing to do virtual family sessions in which you and your teen can have sessions virtually instead of going into the office. Even more, you can also use virtual sessions to discuss concerns you may have, ask questions, or make suggestions about topics discussed in therapy.

You'll want to ask about the possibility of incorporating virtual sessions during the very first session. Virtual sessions truly depend on your therapist's credentials, state regulations, comfort level, and awareness of modern methods for counseling sessions. It has been my experience that most older therapists, typically over the age of 50, tend to rely more on in-person talk therapy than virtual therapy. Some of my older colleagues laugh at the thought of incorporating virtual therapy into their therapeutic style of treating clients. Younger therapists and clients tend to perceive virtual sessions differently. In fact, I tend to use virtual sessions for my less severe clients and for clients who I can see at least 1-2 times per month in-person. Although I used to be "against" the idea, I have grown more knowledgeable about the process and can see the benefits of virtual sessions for many clients. As a provider, I must be aware of changing laws, ethics codes, and insurance regulations. You'll want to check to see if your teen's therapist is able to comfortably provide virtual therapy. Any therapist can claim they understand how to provide virtual therapy, but only a few really know how virtual sessions are supposed to go.

Teens who only want virtual therapy sessions

It is important for you to know that most state regulations require therapists to have some kind of telehealth training or exposure before promoting themselves as virtual therapists. If your teen has a therapist who promotes themselves as a "virtual therapist" I think it would be acceptable to ask them if they offer in-person sessions and if so, if you can alternate between the two. I tend to take this approach with many of my clients. You can also ask about their training and years of experience providing virtual sessions. Although I discourage parents to hit their teen's therapist with a barrage of questions about their training and education, I do believe parents and teens should feel comfortable enough to ask the more sensitive questions when the time is right. Because each state has different regulations for a therapist who may provide virtual therapy services, it is important that parents ask what their training has been with teens who are suicidal so that when/if a crisis or emergency arises, you will have comfort in knowing the therapist knows exactly what to do virtually.

Virtual therapists must truly know what they are doing when working with "high risk" teens who have frequent suicidal thoughts. There is definitely a degree of intuition and common sense that goes into providing virtual therapy. Difficult mental health challenges such as bipolar disorder and chronic suicidal thoughts require a therapist to have a high degree of confidence, skill, and expertise. I encourage you to educate yourself as well to telehealth services and its new impact on the mental health field. Many professional organizations and associations for mental health therapists have been establishing guidelines and standards for providing virtual therapy to clients, especially clients with challenging mental health problems. Other organizations have engaged in promulgating standards useful for assisting many health insurance companies who reimburse mental health providers for virtual sessions (such as Highmark and Cigna Insurance). I do encourage you to contact your insurance company to inquire about coverage for virtual sessions. You'd want to ask if your coverage reimburses for virtual sessions and if there are any resources on their website that you could download to learn more about this service.

According to David Luxton, Eve-Lynn Nelson, and Marlene Maheu (2016) in their book *A Practitioner's Guide to Telemental Health: How to Conduct Legal, Ethical, and Evidence-Based Telepractive*, they explain that:

> "Behavioral health services that are provided via technology also create a different context for the therapeutic process, including uniques benefits and challenges. For example, telepractice extends the reach of service to underserved groups and diverse population that may have had limited previous contact with behavioral health services and/or with technology. Thus, it is crucial for clinicians to be familiar with how to work with clients/patients from diverse backgrounds."

The authors also highlight complications that even I had not considered:

> "...There are also potential complications that can arise during telepractice. For example, the clinician facing a delicate mandated reporting situation must be aware that an emotionally charged conversation with a

client/patient about potential abuse may be more difficult to manage via VC [Virtual Counseling]. Such a client/patient may easily and quickly respond to abuse-related inquiries by simply turning off the computer. Such clients/patients are then unlikely to respond to attempts for further contact.

Working via technology, then, also requires an understanding of how technology alters a professional clinical relationship....Without proper training, clinicians may unwittingly put clients/patients and themselves at risk by treading into new terrain without full understanding and appreciation of these telepractice issues (pp 5-6)."

It is important, then, that you and your teen evaluate your comfort level with virtual sessions and then begin to ask the therapist the necessary questions.

How I prepare a family to use virtual therapy

When I meet with parents and teens together during the very first session I tend to provide an environment that would stimulate the parent to discuss concerns, ask questions, and share their perception of therapy. After the parent speaks I ask the teen if they would like to add anything. If not, I go on to discuss treatment goals and steps needed to achieve them. I also discuss progress and ways parents can help their teen maintain that progress. Once the session draws closer to the end, I use the final 20 to 15 minutes to engage the teen and the parent in a fun therapeutic activity focused on reducing stress, tension, or anxiety. This also allows the teen to experience their parents being present in a more positive way. For many teens, parents often come into the office to discuss their concerns, fears, or disappointment. Rarely does a teen have their parent present to simply play a game or have fun in a session. It's a way to introduce therapy to both the teen and the parent in a different way. Once rapport and trust have been established, the family and I schedule a few sessions throughout the month and choose a time when the teen can engage in virtual therapy uninterrupted. After about 3-4 sessions during the month, I have the teen and the parent return to the office to review treatment goals and sign documentation, discuss challenges or progress, reconnect with me as the provider, and schedule further sessions.

If you are interested in this approach to treatment and believe it may be helpful to your teen, I encourage you to ask your teen's therapist if they would be open to your teen coming to the office at least 1-2 times a month for in-person sessions. You may be able to find a virtual therapist who mixes both virtual and in-person sessions in treatment. Keep in mind that every therapist is different and that the therapist may not see value in this approach. But there is no harm in asking.

Barriers to maintaining treatment with a personality or mood disorder

I have treated my fair share of young women and men with Borderline Personality Disorder (BPD) including teens (male and female) with BPD traits. Although I have not been specifically trained to work with this population, it isn't unlikely for the average therapist to receive a request for services from someone with BPD. What I have learned, over the past 9-10 years working with teens, is that BPD should become a diagnosis for adolescents despite the many years of research claiming this would be a negligent venture for the profession. The reality is that many adolescents, primarily girls, struggle with BPD symptoms all of the time but cannot be diagnosed until age 18. By that time most of the symptoms have worsened and the window of opportunity has the potential of closing by the time the teen reaches "adult age." Recent research suggests that BPD should become a diagnosis for adolescents who are exhibiting many of the traits that adult client's display. I couldn't agree more.

One of the biggest barriers to treatment compliance is high sensitivity to a perceived threat (i.e, abandonment, rejection, or judgment) that many individuals with BPD display in clinical settings. About 2 years ago I received a referral from a psychiatrist who had little to no experience working with teen girls who had traits similar to that of BPD. He referred her to me because of my trauma training and the years of trauma this young woman suffered. When the day of intake finally arrived I was able to meet with this young lady. She was a teenager who had been raised in a very invalidating and emotionally unavailable household. She was removed from the home of her biological parents after being found by the police to be living in a drug infested, dilapidated, and unsafe home environment in an inner city area of Chicago. She was brought to my office after years of therapy in Chicago with various therapists, behavior specialists, and psychiatrists. A trauma therapist was her "last hope" according to her psychiatrist. I accepted the referral and decided to treat and target the negative impact of the trauma she had experienced. Little did I know, I would also need to treat the unspecified mood disorder (i.e., unspecified as a result of a complex battery of symptoms) and the borderline personality traits. This is when I realized that a team approach is needed to treat BPD.

Sadly, this client ended up intentionally withholding information from her psychiatrist. Although she had worked through a tremendous amount of trauma, her BPD symptoms seemed to be intensifying. Not only had she robbed a neighbor of $400 worth of merchandise and thought it was funny, but she also began to drink and drive which resulted in her acquiring a DUI charge. Because of her age and the fact that she had not been in trouble before, she was placed on house-arrest and later probation. This resulted in a criminal record and months of remediation and counseling for substance abuse. She ended up lying to her psychiatrist about "making progress" as she had continued to steal and drink alcohol, even while on probation. She then impulsively terminated her treatment from her psychiatrist. This led to medication noncompliance and major conduct issues. Without her medication refills and a refusal to seek out a new psychiatrist (even with my referral and willingness to set it up for her), she became psychotic and paranoid. I eventually 302'd her (i.e., involuntarily committed her to the hospital) for further treatment. She was kept for 2 weeks and referred to an intensive outpatient program that would provide therapy 3 times a week for 6 weeks while allowing her to work, attend school, and go home. As for me, I provided her parents with resources and information for care after the completion of her IOP program and closed her case. I was unable to maintain her care due to oppositional, defiant, impulsive, and reckless behaviors that jeopardized her safety and the safety of others.

The treatmemt course of individuals with BPD is complicated for a variety of reasons not limited to: mood lability, splitting (i.e., black/white) and rigit thinking patterns, sensitivity to rejection, fear of abandonment (real or perceived), psychotic symptoms or paranoia under stress, suicidal or homicidal threats (including passive death wishes), dishonesty or deliberate withholding, overt or covert threats to continuity of care, attention-seeking, impulsivity (i.e., acting before thinking, making rash decisions, displaying emotional reactivity), self-destructive or self-injurious behaviors (i.e., cutting, burning, etc), and dysregulation of mood and affect. Teens with BPD may display a pattern of behaviors that come across as oppositional, defiant, and rebellious. They come across as individuals who want nothing to do with others and who would feel much better if they committed suicide or self-destructed in some fashion. Many of these teens display behavior patterns that I discussed in the beginning of the book which I have termed "push-and-pull" behavior. It appears as if they want help, emotional support, or attention but then, on the other hand, they display behaviors that push others away. If the teen is also depressed, BPD symptoms can worsen.

Treating teenagers with BPD symptoms can seem like one of the most difficult (and sometimes impossible) things to do. There are so many influences in the lives of teens that it can seem impossible trying to narrow down the "cause" of the dysfunctional thought processes, emotions, and behaviors. These teens rarely learn from experience and find themselves being held hostage by their impulsive behaviors. Things do become more complicated when the teen's moods become uncontrollably labile.

Barriers to maintaining treatment with moody teens

Most parents struggle with teens who refuse to open up about their feelings, their thoughts, and their darkest secrets. Sadly, for many teenagers, their deepest darkest secret is suicidal thoughts. For these teenagers exposing their darkest secret means being vulnerable and trusting the person they are revealing their thoughts too. For many teens this can seem too vulnerable so they retreat into a world of depression, isolation, and aloneness. Maintaining treatment with these teenagers can be one of the most difficult things a parent (and therapist) may have to face. Teenagers with BPD traits, oppositional defiant disorder, or mood disorders struggle the most with revealing their thought patterns and feelings. Teenagers with BPD traits may display what I call a "push and pull" mood and attitude. The push-and-pull mood/attitude consists of the teenager going back and forth (like a seesaw) with attitudes, beliefs, moods, and feelings. This is often quite characteristic of adults with borderline personality disorder. For example, I once counseled a young woman who struggled not only with BPD but also major depressive disorder with psychotic features. In other words, this young lady displayed BPD as well as depression that included hallucinations, delusions, and paranoia. This young lady came to sessions in a positive mood but during the course of the session would immediately change. She exhibited multiple attitudes, beliefs, and feelings on the same topic over the course of almost an entire year. On one occasion in which her mother and father were present for the session, she would begin to cry as she discussed how severely depressed and paranoid she was. However, she would also get very irritable and angry with her father and mother for wanting to hug her in session, show their emotional support, and offer words of encouragement. Although it seemed like she was emotionally hurting and craving affection, she actually wanted everybody including me to leave her alone. During some sessions in which she was highly emotional and struggled to control her negative self-talk, she appeared as if she wanted me to show her attention and yet at the same time would distance herself from me. The moment I would attempt to reach out to her in compassion and empathy, she would slam the door completely by withdrawing and shutting down. I soon found out that this "push and pull" attitude was quite characteristic of teens with BPD traits and depressive symptoms. In fact, this "hot and cold" attitude is also characteristic of some teens who have chronic suicidal thoughts. I often tell parents, and want to remind you, that a "hot and cold" or "push and pull" attitude tends to be a symptom (rather than a fleeting mood) of the complex symptomatology of BPD and a mood disorder. Unfortunately, teens who are struggling with suicidal ideation, gestures, or behaviors may find reaching out for help extremely difficult because of this "push and pull," personality. It is sad for me to watch an intelligent adolescent struggle to understand why their behaviors are pushing everyone away from them including therapy.

When I started counseling during a 2-year-long internship in a reputable psychiatric hospital and teaching university, a male patient on the ward would turn suicidal the moment staff would reach out to him in compassion. I found this behavior quite perplexing as an intern. It took months of consultation with experienced clinicians for me to finally understand the complexity of his mind and emotions. When he was not getting attention from others on the ward, he would be very discontent. At other times when he was getting attention on the ward, he was content. The moment I would comment on how much progress he had made he would instantly turn sullen, depressed, and even suicidal. It was as if he couldn't exist or have an identity aside from his depressed, angry, and suicidal persona. As an inexperienced clinician at the time, I was not prepared for this contradictory behavior. However, I soon learned that many suicidal teens with BPD show similar behavioral patterns. When such behavior is exhibited in teens about therapy, maintaining treatment becomes extremely difficult. Such teens may verbally express they are "better" or feeling "stable," and yet, go home and attempt suicide. Other teens, especially those who have bipolar disorder, may become suicidal as they cycle into mania or hypomania. Interestingly, research suggests that some teens who are depressed may attempt suicide when they are actually feeling better (National Center For Health Research, 2017). According to the Child Mind Institute (2017), teens who take some antidepressants, primarily the SSRI's (Selective Serotonin Reuptake Inhibitors) may begin to experience suicidal ideations but that doesn't include all teens. When the "black-box" warning from the FDA (Food & Drug Administration) came out in 2004 about the correlation between SSRI's and suicidal thoughts, parents panicked and became leery of psychiatrists who would prescribe them. While it is important to keep in mind that some antidepressants may not be effective with your teen, "moody teens" may respond well to them. If you suspect that your teen's antidepressant is doing the complete opposite of helping them, I encourage you to reach out to the doctor who prescribed them. If you don't have a doctor, contact your PCP.

Teens who struggle with BPD traits and mood disorders can be very complicated in clinical settings. It is important that you, as the parent, understand the contradictory and perplexing behaviors that can often emerge in suicidal teens. These symptoms can make keeping your teen in treatment very difficult. Open communication with everyone who is involved with your teen will be essential to your teen's healing.

Maintaining open communication with your teen's school

Open communication with your teen's school can sometimes be a challenge. Trying to connect your teen's therapist to their teacher can also be a challenge. The most important step is getting your teen on board with allowing you to connect their therapist to their school. Some teens prefer their school not know they are struggling or having problems outside of academic challenges. Some reasons include but are not limited to: fear of information getting out to other kids or teachers, judgment or discrimination, and embarrassment. In cases such as these, it may be helpful to normalize the need for help, encourage your teen to reach out for support, and model reaching out to others for support yourself. If we can't tell teens how they should approach the world, we can model it for them. If you do decide not to involve the school, you have that right.

Staying connected to your teen's school will include finding a "point person" to talk to about your concerns and receive updates on your teen's performance. I encourage the parent to send a monthly email or leave a voicemail about their teen to a "point person" at the school such as a teacher, school counselor, or Principal. You may want to do the same to ensure you and the teacher are on the same page. It might be a good idea for you and your teen to pay a visit to the school counselor or school psychologist to request further support while your teen is at school. If you are looking for other mental health services in the area your school counselor/psychologist should have a listing of local therapists, psychologists, psychiatrists, and other mental health professionals you can contact. In some cases, the school counselor/psychologist has already collaborated with a mental health professional from a local agency on other students. So their access to external resources may be broader than yours. For example, when I worked in a rural group private practice seeing children and teens I had become very close to the school counselors in the area. Many of the school counselors would refer students to me and I would refer students to them. It was a great way to keep the doors of communication open and support the students.

When you don't want to rely on the school

I have encountered parents who did not trust or like their teen's school counselor/psychologist. In cases such as these, it may be necessary for you to contact your insurance company and ask them to refer you to a listing of local mental health professionals. You can also ask your primary care physician for a referral or list of mental health professionals. You may be able to find information online through your insurance company. If not, you can call the number on the back of your card that says "member services." If that doesn't turn out to be the best avenue for you, you can search for a therapist online yourself. You can do a quick Google search for your area or you can go to www.psychologytoday.com and navigate to "Find a therapist" search box and put in your zip code. You will find yours truly there and many other therapists. The only thing I would caution you about is relying 100% on therapist profiles. You may want to schedule an appointment or consultation as a way to explore "fit" before making any commitments with the therapist. You may find value in asking your teen to take a look at the therapist profiles to give them independence and choice in setting up an appointment. Most therapist profiles also include a photo with examples of their therapeutic style. Involving your teen in this process may make pursuing therapy a bit easier for them. It also provides an opportunity for you and your teen to work together. The last thing you would want is for your teen to ask why you didn't ask them if they wanted to see a particular therapist after having scheduled an appointment.

You may be the "boss" in your family but your teen should have the right to choose who they want to talk to. I find that when teens are given a choice, they tend to commit to therapy more readily.

Staying organized

Staying organized can be very challenging. For some families, the teen may be seeing multiple therapists, treatment specialists, and doctors. It can be difficult trying to keep everyone's name straight, every appointment marked, and every recommendation in mind. That being said, you must find a way to organize yourself and your teen's treatment information. When I meet with parents who bring their younger children (ages 3-10) to me for therapy, I include a brief conversation about staying organized and offer to provide some tips. Below I offer 6 things you can do to ensure you remain organized:

- **Put all appointment where you can see them:** One teen told me that their family kept all of their appointments on a whiteboard on the refrigerator, in mom and dad's phone, in the car on post-it notes, and on their individual computers. There was no way they were going to forget a session. Put reminders in more than one place.

- **Encourage your teen to set reminders:** Even though you may have reminders on your own phone or in your own planner, your teen can add an alarm or reminder to their phone too. This not only teaches them to prioritize what's important, but it also may give them a sense of responsibility when it comes to attending sessions.

- **Keep a therapy binder:** When I worked with adolescents in a group therapy environment, I encouraged them to create a binder where they could put all of the artwork, worksheets, notes, articles, assignments or "homework," and certificates or rewards received. The binders were created in the group and each teen was able to make the binder something special for themselves. The final product was amazing! The binders looked great, the teens had a certain level of pride associated with their own creations, and all of their therapy related information was kept organized.

- **Keep a file drawer or folder specifically for therapy:** I once counseled a young mother who brought all 3 of her girls to see me for therapy. I remember she brought one of the girls on the wrong day and informed me that "I just got confused." This happened on a few occasions so we put our heads together and came up with a plan. The plan was for her to keep a small, folding file folder with therapy worksheets, artwork, copies of prescriptions, copies of test results, copies of self-report scales, and written down appointments in a safe place at her house. It seemed to do wonders for her and I both.

- **Color code things:** It may be helpful to use different colors for separating appointments or filing away therapy related articles, books, or things received from your teen's appointment(s).

- **Ask your therapist to file away your teen's work:** Some therapists keep every single thing they do in therapy with your teen. But others do not. Some shred the material believing that it will waste space. I don't see anything wrong with you asking your teen's therapist to keep copies of some of the worksheets, self-report assessments, or other clinical files sent home in your teen's therapy file. I once gave a worksheet to a teen client I had but didn't keep a copy. When it came time for me to terminate therapy based on the teen's progress, I couldn't find the work we did in one of the most important sessions we had because I failed to keep a copy of the worksheet for myself. You are not only helping to ensure your teen has a backup copy, but perhaps even the therapist!

Putting it all together

Helping a teen maintain treatment can be a difficult task for a parent. Teens are challenging. But there are ways to encourage your teen to stay in treatment. You can have a mature conversation with them about the consequences of dropping out of care or refusing to follow treatment recommendations. Consequences may include: continued failing grades, being expelled from school or suspended, a declining reputation (especially if negative behaviors are interfering with relationships) loss of extracurricular activities if they do not follow your rules and loss of other privileges. You certainly do not want to come across as authoritarian and make your teen feel as if you are forcing them into therapy. But you do want to be firm and help them understand that treatment is a serious necessity.

If you are struggling with keeping your teen in treatment, it may be helpful to consult with family, close and trusted friends, your teen's teacher and therapist before allowing them to stop treatment or reduce the number of times they attend sessions. I often recommend for my teens to drop down to once or twice a month before stopping completely. This allows a "test run" and affords me and my client the opportunity to process things as they slowly regain their independence.

Teenagers who have a history of suicidal ideation or attempts should take at least a month to two months to slowly come away from therapy. Your teenager may fight you on this because they may feel they're ready to stop therapy sessions, feel the process is taking too long to end, or they may feel very frustrated with therapy and just want to get it over with. Despite how they may feel, it is a really good idea to help them see therapy through to the end. If your teen has a good and caring therapist and has a history of suicidal thoughts, they should be made to remain in treatment (at least for a short duration such as 1 month or 2 months). Any amount of time is better than no time at all. However, if your teen is completely resistant and refuses to engage at all, therapy should be ended. There is no therapeutic value in trying to maintain therapy to a point of making your teen angry or resentful. The most important part of this process is to help your teen see that they need support and that they need to maintain treatment as much as possible. If you are struggling to get your teen to understand this, I encourage you to seek out your own therapy so that you can learn how to best support your teen.

NOTES

Conclusion

Chapter 8

"Parenting is the easiest thing in the world to have an opinion about, but the hardest thing in the world to do."

- Matt Walsh

My mother used to tell me all the time just how difficult parenting is. As a teenager, I would think to myself "I believe parenting is difficult too but perhaps my mom is pessimistic and concerned that I will jump into parenthood too quickly." As I grew in my career and work with many families, I saw exactly what she meant. I would then hear other women say similar things. At this stage in my life, I find that when I meet with a parent who is concerned about the health and wellness of their teen I have great sympathy for them. It is hard. It is trying. It is scary. It is complicated. My job is to ensure you feel supported and have the right information needed for helping your teen get help for suicidal thoughts. I can only imagine the emotional distress you must feel after learning that your teen is considering suicide. Many parents, like yourself, question their parenting style and techniques, question God, question the educational system and even look for others to blame (knowingly or unknowingly). The reality is a bit much to handle and it is only normal that you feel lost, confused, and thrown off. In fact, your teen may have seemed happy, engaged, and healthy to you and others. So what went wrong? We must keep in mind as adults that adolescence is a time of mood lability and fleeting emotions and thoughts. We must also keep in mind that teens, who have mental health challenges, may vary in how they see and feel about life on a daily (sometimes hourly) level. It's a normal process for teens. But this normal process requires parents and teachers to become more knowledgeable about the subtle signs of mental health challenges and the emotional and psychological pain most adolescents experience in today's world.

The role of teachers in preventing teen suicide and raising awareness

I remember asking a group of parents during a seminar on trauma and mental illness if they thought their teen's teacher could help prevent suicide. The results were rather disturbing as many parents felt teachers should be highly responsible for alerting a parent to a teen who is suicidal. Some stated this is true because that's where teens spend the majority of their time. Others stated that teachers are mandated reporters for abuse and should be reporters for suicide too. Is this fair? Some may think yes and others may think no. For me, I believe teachers should be fully trained (on an annual basis) by mental health professionals, certified individuals, or large organizations on the topic of teen suicide. Teachers cannot prevent suicide or raise awareness if they are uninformed about it. So the first step is to ensure people with authority in the lives of teens are educated. Secondly, it will be important for parents to learn how to reach out to teachers to inform them that a teen is struggling with mental health challenges or suicidal thoughts. A lot of parents shy away from this for fear of being judged, for fear of information getting out to others within the community, and/or being judged by the teacher to be a "bad parent." We certainly need to get past this barrier.

The Suicide Prevention Resource Center (2012) created a document that speaks directly to the role of teachers in suicide prevention and awareness. They outline the following as essential to students who may be at risk for contemplation of suicide:

> "Teachers can also play an active role in suicide prevention by fostering the emotional well-being of all students, not just those already at high risk. Teachers are well positioned to promote a feeling of connectedness and belonging in the school community. According to the CDC (2009), school connectedness is the belief by students that adults and peers in the school care about them as individuals as well as about their learning. Connectedness is an important factor in improving academic achievement and healthy behaviors, and it is also specifically related to reductions in suicidal thoughts and attempts (Resnick et al., 1997; Blum et al., 2002)."

Teachers not only play an important role in the nurturance of student well-being but they also play an active role in educating parents about behavioral or mood changes they observe in a throughout the school day. Although teachers are not trained mental health professionals, they are an active part of the teen's daily life and may see signs of mental health or behavioral health problems before parents do. Teachers may also have greater access to a wide selection of resources for supporting teens than a parent does.

Teachers have direct access to community resources and can play an important role in connecting students to community supports that can greatly benefit them such as:
- After school programs
- Wraparound or behavioral support programs
- Mental health counselors
- Vocational counselors
- Big Brother or Big Sister programs
- Educational support services
- Tutoring
- Support groups for teens
- Artistic, musical, or social skills programs or classes within the community

The list is endless. Teachers can be viewed as bridges from the most important setting in a teen's life (i.e. school) to another structured or stable place to learn and evolve. Because of the strong influence teachers have on the lives of suffering teens, I often encourage teachers to:

- Stay involved with the family if a teen becomes suicidal and document every encounter with the teen, family, and treatment providers. Date, time, and content of discussion and outcome should be listed including how you reacted.

- Follow up as necessary and document this.

- Offer emotional, social, and community support by offering to meet with the teen and family, offering resources, or encouraging therapy or support groups.

- Suggest counseling and psychotherapy. Teachers play a major role in connecting families to resources.

- Have a crisis hotline available.

As stated above, teachers play a major role in connecting families to resources within their communities. Teachers can be very influential in the lives of families. As a parent, you have the right to reach out to your teen's therapist or school for local referrals to community-based or counseling programs in the area.

Facts about teens who are at-risk for suicide

As stated above, teachers are in a powerful position to ensure teens who are struggling reach out for help. When I counsel teachers on how to support teens contemplating suicide, I often encourage teachers to keep in mind the following facts:

- Teens who have a history of attempted suicide will most likely have another suicide attempt in the future. Research suggests that attempted suicide is a major risk factor for future attempts.

- Alcohol and drug abuse can contribute to how teens view suicide and can also cause disinhibition or impulsivity. Teens who are using drugs or alcohol may feel less inhibited and more "courageous" or "willing" to engage in harming or killing themselves.

- BPD traits can lead to unstable relationships, poor self-image, repeat suicide attempts, self-injurious behaviors, and impulsivity that all can result in more suicidal gestures or behaviors. The reason for this may be due to a combination of genetics and environment, primarily during development in an unstable childhood. It may also be due to the disorder's chronic symptom of emotional sensitivity.

- Teens who have experienced trauma are also more likely than other teens to engage in self-harming behaviors or have suicidal thoughts. Teens with Post Traumatic Stress Disorder (PTSD) also have suicidal thoughts and may attempt suicide if their symptoms are untreated. For many of these teens, suicidal gestures or behaviors may serve as a temporary band-aid for untreated emotional and psychological pain.

- Access to a means to kill oneself (i.e., drugs, pills, a gun, etc) also increases the possibility that a teen might complete suicide.

- Suicidal behavior is often greater for individuals who have more than one risk factor (Adapted from Rodgers 2011 and SPRC 2008). For example, teens who have been sexually abused, have experimented with drugs or alcohol, have dropped out of high school, has an untreated mental illness, and doesn't have a stable household will most likely be more vulnerable to thoughts of suicide and attempted suicide than teens who come from more stable environments. Protective factors (i.e., parental education, socio-economic status, healthy parenting skills, healthy state of mind, etc) can buffer teens from the influence of risk factors (ie, parental substance abuse, poor education, and employment, lack of positive parent-child relationship, etc).

- Challenges at school and difficulties at home can contribute to suicidal thoughts. In fact, teens who have BPD traits may struggle a lot with minimal structure in the home and in the school environment. For example, a teen with BPD who is struggling at home with divorcing parents and is entering the 9th grade, may begin to feel hopeless or helpless and respond by talking about suicide, thinking about suicide, and then acting on them. It is important that teachers view teens from a holistic perspective, taking care to consider any external stressors the student may be struggling with (i.e., divorce, a new baby, bullying, abuse, trauma, a break-up, confusion over self-identity, substance abuse, medical conditions, untreated mental health conditions, etc).

- It is important to conclude this section by reminding teachers that teens who have negative risk factors may or may not be affected by them. In other words, a teen who has many of the above challenges may be able to overcome them with the right amount of support. Teens who come from single-parent households may not struggle with substance abuse, suicidal thoughts, depression, anxiety, or other challenges. With a supportive mother, grandmother, and school environment, the teen may be able to overcome their challenges. Teachers should take care in how they view their students and strive to avoid ideologies that could lead to a self-fulfilling prophecy.

Personality disorders and suicide

According to a fact sheet about mental health created by the University of Washington (2017), "people with personality disorders are approximately three times as likely to die by suicide than those without. Between 25% and 50% of these individuals also have a substance abuse disorder or major depressive disorder." In fact, individuals with BPD tend to struggle with suicidal ideations that may result in multiple gestures and attempts. Because of the relational instability often characteristic of those diagnosed with BPD, black and white thinking or polarized thinking may lead to the individual contemplating suicide as a remedy for negative emotions and thought patterns. For example, I once counseled a 17-year-old (who would clearly meet criteria for BPD) who struggled with every single relationship in his life. He had a negative relationship with his parents and extended family, his school and teachers, his friends and superiors. He came to me for an assessment to confirm or disconfirm BPD because "I just don't think I have the disorder because I don't cut and I don't act crazy." After months of psychotherapy and observation of his actions, interactions, and thoughts about other people in this world, I finally recognized that this young man's BPD showed up more in his very rigit view of humans which was very (black/white, all or nothing) with no gray. He idealized people for a certain period of time and then devalued them the minute they would reject his advances. His inappropriately intense anger would also push others away because almost every argument would end with him threatening to kill himself. His personality disorder made every single relationship in his life unnecessarily difficult. The unnecessary difficulty he created led him to contemplate and even attempt suicide on multiple occasions. Although I cannot conclude that his behaviors would be any different without his BPD, I do believe that his personality disorder made it difficult for him to emotionally connect with others and made it all too easy for him to resort to drastic measures like suicide when things would not go his way.

    Even more, I once counseled a 19-year-old female who displayed a very immature persona for her age. She loved "hello kitty" and would engage with younger teens in online forums about the caricature. Her fascination with "hello kitty" was alarming, to say the least. Instead of accepting invitations to adult events, she would decline them so that she could retreat to the world of "hello kitty" and remain separate from the adult responsibilities she desperately avoided. There was often no "in-between" for her. She was either a very young child on a psychological and emotional level or a very wild young adult. This regression or decline occurred after about 3 months in treatment. It is not uncommon for individuals diagnosed with BPD to decline or regress during the treatment process. At times, this regression is a sign that treatment needs to shift and/or expectations and boundaries need to be re-established.

On multiple occasions, during sessions, she would burst into tears while discussing the "party-girl" weekend she had which often led to unsolicited sexual encounters, promiscuity, binge-drinking, and encounters with police. She not only developed a substance abuse disorder and a criminal record, but multiple thoughts of suicide which led to several attempts while intoxicated. Any attempt from her family to "rescue" her resulted in a suicide attempt. When her family would back off from her, she would resort to her world of "hello kitty." There was often a "back and forth," "push and pull" nature to her. This created much instability and confusion within many of her relationships. Because she could never maintain a healthy and positive relationship, her suicidal thoughts intensified. After months of counseling her with little to no progress, I re-engaged her in a very serious conversation (which had occurred weeks prior to this period) about her personality disorder and the symptoms (i.e., mainly the suicidal gestures and attempts) that keep others at a distance from her. She was very blinded to the fact that her suicidal ideations, gestures, and attempts kept people from wanting anything to do with her. To make matters worse, this young lady also struggle with recurrent, severe major depressive disorder which is a "risk factor" for suicidal thoughts and attempts.

The takeaway is that personality disorders tend to complicate the clinical picture and makes treatment of suicidal thoughts and behaviors more difficult. Research suggests that BPD is the only diagnosis with suicide as part of the diagnostic criteria. In other words, suicidal thoughts, gestures, or behaviors are a "symptom" of BPD. In a way, this emphasizes the chronic nature of suicidal thoughts, gestures, and behaviors in BPD and also highlights the challenges facing clients and providers when BPD is apart of the clinical conceptualization or picture.

It is important that if parents or teachers suspect that a teen may be exhibiting signs of a personality disorder that they encourage the teen to seek out psychotherapy. Psychotherapy isn't always successful with individuals who have personality disorders because, for the most part, individuals with personality disorders do not believe they have a problem. However, in the case of BPD, because of suicidal thoughts or behaviors, relational instability, impulsivity, and emotional lability, the individual tends to become more open to treatment when they begin to suffer the consequences of their disorder. In other words, when symptoms create so much disturbance or distress that normal functioning is difficult, the individual becomes more open to the self-exploration of psychotherapy.

Treatment compliance may be difficult due to the client's lack of trust, habitual relationship challenges, impulsivity, boundary-pushing, low self-esteem, splitting, triangulating, negative thought patterns, generalization, and black/white thinking patterns. Clients with BPD may oscillate between idealizing the therapist and hating the therapist. Manipulation, displayed by some individuals with BPD, may also create barriers in the therapeutic relationship. As a result, teens with BPD traits may completely reject psychotherapy and refuse to be compliant. It is important that you are prepared for this possibility and know what to do ahead of time.

When attempts at communication fail with resistant teens

Have you ever attempted to have a serious discussion with a teen only to later find out that they weren't listening to you in the first place? Don't feel bad about yourself. Teens are difficult. It isn't easy to determine how a teen will respond to attempts at helping them. When your teen rejects you or something unexpected happens, it is important to revisit the conversation at a time when you are alone and can ask yourself if you did anything you should apologize for. It will also be helpful to evaluate if you could have broached the topic differently. Once you examine your own approach you may find it helpful to ask your teen why they are reluctant to hear you or appreciate your concern. If the teen meets criteria for a personality disorder such as BPD there really isn't much you can do outside of suggesting psychotherapy. Most teens with BPD personality traits push back, argue, and dig their heels in.

In other situations, triangulation may occur. When this happens, two or more people get involved and things blow up. It is important you learn of some of the reactions teens may have to you broaching the topic of suicide. Triangulation can be defined as any behavior that misleads, confuses, or damages the relationship between the communicator and more than one other person. Triangulation is a tactic someone may use to control, manipulate, misinform, or deceive.

Triangulation is not always an intentional behavior. It may be unintentional, especially if the teen is sharing what happened with a trusted friend, parent, or another individual in their life.

Preparation for communication is the best way to ensure you are ready for whatever may come your way when you decide to broach the topic of suicide. The best way to ensure you are ready for your teen's reaction is to educate yourself about suicide. Know what teens talk about. You can also talk to other teens about this topic, reach out to your local mental health support group for suggestions or guidance (e.g., National Alliance on Mental Illness), talk with the teen's primary care physician (PCP), or ask for a free consultation with a mental health professional experienced with treating suicidal teens. When broaching the topic of suicide with resistant teens, be ready for them to only listen to respond. Teens are really good at completely dismissing or not hearing what you are trying to get across to them. Teens can also be so bent on getting you to see their own point of view that they fail to pay attention to yours. A teen who listens to respond will not hear anything you are saying while simultaneously trying, very hard, to get you to hear them out. Drop the conversation for a later time or when you can come up with a better plan. In most cases, it is often better to "roll with the resistance," according to Miller & Rollnick, 2002. **Motivational Interviewing (MI)** is a person-centered, yet directive approach to counseling resistant clients. The goal of MI is to reduce resistance and ambivalence and increase compliance or growth in therapy. It is a collaborative approach that involves the client in treatment. Therapy doesn't move forward without the client. MI is used to help clients open up, become active participants in their treatment, and make needed changes. Principles of MI can be very helpful in getting teens to open up about their suicidal thoughts, gestures, and behaviors. I encourage you to learn more about this approach and try some of the techniques you learn.

The Principles of MI include:
- Rolling with the resistance
- Expressing empathy
- Avoiding argumentation or confrontation
- Developing discrepancy (i.e., the idea that change can happen when there is a discrepancy between the current behavior and the ultimate goal)
- Supporting self-efficacy

Although MI is often helpful to clinicians, it may not be helpful or even interesting to you. Therefore, I encourage you to practice your reaction or response to some of the following typical patterns of teen behavior:

- **Using emotions to control:** Some teens are so dramatic that they could be diagnosed with histrionic personality traits which are traits I have seen about four times out of the nine years I have worked in the field of psychology. Histrionic personality traits can include the following: exaggerated claims, exaggerated tone of voice and actions, theatrical tones of voice or behaviors, rapid change of vocal tones, dramatic expressions, and seductive behaviors. It can be very difficult to identify a histrionic personality because of co-occurring disorders (i.e., BPD, bipolar disorder, substance use disorder, etc) and even environmental influences (i.e., how the person was raised, role models or adult influences, etc). But you will notice when speaking with a teen who can be exaggerative that he/she will sometimes use exaggerated emotions to distract or appear as the victim. It's simply manipulative.

- **Studying others and anticipating certain reactions:** I once counseled a teenager, age 17, who was very, very skilled at getting social cues and being sarcastic. He had a way that he would create a discussion (among his friends or family, sometimes even his teachers) and once everyone would become emotionally charged or hyper-focused on the topic, he would "back out." He would then watch reactions, changes in emotions, and listen for cues of anger. He was "studying" his family and social group. When he wanted something such as a girlfriend or a car, he would know what buttons to push and how. He developed a reputation for using others to teach him how to manipulate and get over on them. He appeared to be ready for every encounter with an adult.

- **Rehearsing lines in anticipation of an**

encounter with an adult: It has been long thought that if a teen is calm when they are being approached by an adult, they are accepting of the encounter and are being cooperative. But research suggests that the calmer the person, the higher the probability that the person may be lying or may have traits of a sociopath. Why? Because when you "rehearse" what you are going to say and the arguments you are going to use, you are calm. Why get bent out of shape?

- **Manipulating others into "playing" roles:** Triangulation creates three kinds of roles: victim ("poor me"), persecutor ("it's all your fault"), and rescuer ("help me"). A manipulative teen who knows exactly how to push people into such roles (often creating chaos and mistrust among the victims), has learned how to keep adults far away from their vulnerabilities. Although most teens who meet criteria for BPD may not display these behaviors, we cannot ignore the fact that some individuals with BPD utilize this pattern of communication to get their needs met.

- **Becoming seductive:** Manipulators are really good at being seductive, especially if they are physically attractive or have some kind of "prestige." It is important to be ready for the teen who may manipulate using their appearance, their language or terminology, and even their intelligence and social astuteness.

- **Exaggerating minor details to distract or derail the encounter:** Teens who are resistant to adults and skilled at manipulation will often exaggerate details to distract your attention away from the elephant in the room. They may also overreact when confronted about their suicidal thoughts, gestures, or behaviors.

Communication with teens can be very stressful. Know

how you are going to react, how you are going to calm an emotional storm or argument, and how you are going to end it if need be. Just be prepared.

Why I believe integrating faith is a good start

I was raised by a single mother who was fully devoted to God. She was displeased by religious ideologies and formal practices that did nothing more than satisfy a need for perfection and communal identity. After introducing scripture to me at around 10 or 11-years-old, I began to pursue scripture on my own in search of a true God. By the time I got to college, I began to study psychology, religion, law, and philosophy. All four subjects shared a common thread. The common thread was a search for meaning in a world where meaning is hard to find. In a world full of mystery, these disciplines attempted to integrate spirituality into a society fully engulfed by scientific "truths," engrained values, and loose belief systems. At the time I couldn't understand why psychology, religion, law, and philosophy separated except for the fact that religion and philosophy embraces "what ifs" and possibilities, while law and psychology embraces "absolutes." Despite learning about this short-sided and limited view of human nature, I began to see how the basic principles of my Christian faith and embracing of God's principles informed my work with clients.

When working with some of my clients I tend to unravel the principles of my faith down to its basic form so that all I see (and all my client sees) are sound principles infused by God. Despite various interpretations, Jesus was a leader of the faith. I believe He performed miracles and healings that were unexplainable. I believe there is a supernatural power to faith and, when exercised, can break down barriers, move mountains, and re-wire the human spirit. Because of these things I strongly believe that faith has a place in psychotherapy.

It's interesting to read the Bible and see that many of the principles and ethics of psychology can also be found in scripture. Such principles include but are not limited to:

- Selflessness
- Harmony and togetherness
- Teamwork and cooperation
- Peace and faith
- Gratitude and thankfulness

- Perseverance and motivation
- Pushing past trial and tribulation
- Rebuilding of faith after loss of hope
- Servanthood or a willingness to help and serve others
- Graciousness
- Forgiveness and truth

These are powerful and extremely significant for healing. It is also significant for a therapist to display these principles as well. If this is the case, why then do we remain closed-minded to the potential power of religion in therapy work? Why then do we remain oblivious to the power of faith in a teen's life? Sadly, we have been influenced by the unnecessary fear attached to years of political pressure (and group-think) inherent in the fields of psychology, philosophy, law and religion. But I'm a firm believer that there is an unexplored powerful correlation between these disciplines. I choose to incorporate the value of faith and Christianity in counseling. It's amazing just how much a teen can grow by knowing they are cared for, loved unconditionally, accepted, not alone, and supported. If you see value in this approach to counseling for your teen, I encourage you to reach out to a counselor who has knowledge of spiritual things and lives their life based on the principles of their spiritual knowledge. I often tell parents that when a teen is struggling with existential questions, the pursuit of raw unconditional acceptance by an informed therapist is key.

Christians suffer depression & suicidal thoughts too
Faith-based communities are a natural environment for fostering positive relationships and interactions. Although it can open the door for positive experiences, it can also lead individuals to negative self-talk, reduced self-esteem, guilt, avoidance of God, and depression and suicide as a result of isolating or withdrawing. Teenagers are particularly vulnerable to this as they are in the process of developing an identity and self-image. A weak or "broken" self-image is likely to worsen in overly religious churches, organizations, and even families. For example, a teen who is struggling with his or her identity may begin to feel discouraged by the concept of "meeting God's exectations" when feeling depressed or suicidal. Many of the teens I have spoken with end up leaving the church for fear of disappointing God or not meeting his expectations. Without a fully

developed self-image or identity, these teens fail to realize that it isn't God who is disappointed in them, but possibly the people who say they represent Him. Teens who are suicidal may also find themselves feeling "ousted" by the religious environment in which they exist. They may find sharing of their suicidal thoughts difficult for fear of being rejected or psycho-analyzed by the head of the church or organization. Some religious environments hold the belief that having suicidal thoughts are "unlike Christians" because Christians should have faith. This is a detrimental belief system. In fact, if you analyze scripture and study the men who represented God in both the New and Old Testament, you will find that many of the men of the Bible displayed depression, anxiety, uncertainty, fear, loneliness, and even suicidal thoughts. It is a normal part of human existence and suffering. The prophet Elijah (found in 1 Kings 19) asked God to take his life as a result of feeling overwhelmed, ousted, and depressed. He ran for miles, found a juniper tree, and "collapsed" in fatigue asking that God would take his life (1 Kings chapter 19, verses 3-5).

The Apostle Paul also struggled with feelings of defeat and exhaustion:

"...I have worked much harder, been in prison more frequently, been flogged more severely, and been exposed to death again and again. Five times I received from the Jews the forty lashes minus 1. Three times I was beaten with rods, once I was pelted with stones, three times I was shipwrecked. I spent a night and a day in the open sea, I have been constantly on the move. I have been in danger from rivers, in danger from bandits, in danger from my fellow Jews, in danger from Gentiles, in danger in the city, in danger in the country, in danger at sea, and in danger from false believers. I have labored and toiled and have often gone without sleep; I have known hunger and thirst and have often gone without food; I have been cold and naked. Besides everything else, I face daily the pressure of my concern for all the churches...." (*2 Corinthians chapter 11, verses 16-33. New International Version*).

Faith is the foundation of hope. Faith reminds us that all things are possible if God allows it. It reminds us that God's strength can far exceed human effort. Faith makes possible what the natural world makes impossible. When someone is struggling with suicidal thoughts, primarily adolescents, we must respond to the call of God by sharing nothing but the truth with them. The truth is that suicidal thoughts are not a sin. They are not rejected by God. God doesn't love the teen any less for having them. In fact, God just may be holding this person closer than we may think. I like Romans 8:38-39 which says:

> "For I am convinced that neither death nor life, neither angels nor demons, neither the present nor the future, nor any powers, neither height or depth, nor anything else in all creation, will be able to separate us from the love of God that is in Christ Jesus our Lord" (New International Version).

It is important that the church spread the true message that the oppressiveness of life and uncertainty does not automatically diminish one's standing with God. In fact, scriptural literature suggests that oppressive forces push us into the arms of God. It is there where we grow. It is there where we find peace. It is there where we find solace. Not judgment, not hate, and not rejection.

Because depression can be very isolating, it is important that sufferers have someone to turn to. It isn't always easy for depressed teens to reach out to a community who promises support, love, and acceptance but doesn't fully show it. That's why Christians must be willing to embrace those who may not want to live. We must show the love of God to those who feel they need it most. We must learn to show unconditional positive regard to those who feel unworthy to receive it. Are you willing to join me in spreading this corrected view of faith? I hope so! Our teens need it. They need it more today than they ever needed it before.

Putting it all together

Understanding your teen can feel like one of the most difficult things you have ever had to do. It will take great patience, knowledge, and strength to help them get through this difficult time in their life. As a parent, you are probably terrified of your teen, terrified about the possibility of recovery, and terrified about their future. I encourage you to consider pursuing therapy or spiritual counseling as you go through this difficult period. Getting therapy also means that you are engaging in self-care and ensuring that you are strong enough (emotionally and psychologically) to cope with your teen's difficulties. A client once said to me "how can I feed the crowd if I don't feed myself?" I find this to be extremely accurate.

I wish you all the best on your journey with your teen. Hold on to faith that things will work out as they were predestined to. No matter how painful, untimely, or challenging things may be, you will overcome.

Wish you and your family all the best,

Tamara Hill

Resources

Suicide resources:

- Suicide Prevention Lifeline: 1-800-273-8255
- American Association of Suicidology www.suicidology.org or @AAsuicidology.
- Suicide Prevention Network www.cspn-rcps.com or @ottprevention.
- Counseling resources:
- www.remedylive.com or @chatlistenlove.
- Pearls 4 Teen Girls www.pearlsforteengirls.com or @PEARLS4TeenGirl.

Book resources

- Calming Your Anxious Child: Words To Say and Things To Do by Kathleen Trainor.
- The Mindfulness Solution For Intense Emotions: Take Control Of Borderline Personality Disorder With DBT by Cedar R Koons.
- Mental Health In A Failed American System by Támara Hill, LPC.

References

American Academy of Pediatrics. (2000). Suicide and suicide attempts in adolescence. Pediatrics 105 (4), 871-876.

American Foundation of Suicide Prevention. (2016). Suicide statistics. Retrieved from https://afsp.org/about-suicide/suicide-statistics/.

American Association of Suicidality. (2016). African American suicide fact sheet based on 2014 data. Retrieved from http://www.suicidology.org/resources/facts-statistics.

American Foundation of Suicide Prevention. (2016). Model school district policy on suicide prevention. Retrieved from https://afsp.org/wp-content/uploads/2016/01/Model-Policy_FINAL.pdf.

Brooks, M., & Barclay, L. (2017). After psychiatric discharge, suicide risk elevated. MedScape. Retrieved from, https://www.medscape.org/viewarticle/882470?nlid=117425_2804&src=wnl_cmemp_170828_mscpedu_psyc&uac=208331FZ&impID=1420672&faf=1.

Beghi, M., & Rosenbaum, JF. (2010). Risk factors for fatal and non-fatal repetition of suicide attempt: A critical appraisal. Current Opinion Psychiatry 23(4), 349-55. doi: 10.1097/YCO.0b013e32833ad783.

Bloom, L. S. (2010). Red Flag Meetings. Retrieved from http://www.sanctuaryweb.com/Portals/0/2010%20PDFs%20NEW/2010%20Bloom%20Red%20Flag%20Meetings.pdf.

Center for Substance Abuse Treatment : SAMHSA/CSAT (1999).

Enhancing motivation for change in substance abuse treatment. Treatment Improvement Protocol (TIP) series, No. 3. Rockvlle (MD): Substance Abuse and Mental Health Services Administration (US); 1999. Report No.: (SMA) 99-3354.

Koplewicz, S. H. (2017). Antidepressants and teen suicides: Untreated depression can be lethal to adolescents.For many medication is a lifeline. Medication. Retrieved from, https://childmind.org/article/antidepressants-and-teen-suicides/.

Mental Health Reporting. (2017). Fact Sheets: Facts about mental illness and suicide. Retrieved from http://depts.washington.edu/mhreport/facts_suicide.php.

Melton, G. J. (n.d.). Heaven's Gate: Religious Group. Encyclopedia Britannica. Retrieved from, https://www.britannica.com/topic/Heavens-Gate-religious-group.

Pennsylvania Department of Education. (n.d). ACT 71. Retrieved from http://www.education.pa.gov/K-12/Safe%20Schools/Pages/Act-71.aspx#tab-1.

PBS New Hour. (2015). Suicide among young American Indians nearly double national rate. Retrieved from, http://www.pbs.org/newshour/rundown/suicide-rate-among-young-american-indians-nearly-double-national-average/.

Sanctuaryweb.com. (2017). The sanctuary model. Retrieved from www.sanctuaryweb.com.

Suicide Prevention Resource Center. (2012). The role of high school teachers in preventing suicide. Retrieved from http://www.sprc.org/sites/default/files/resource-program/V13_HS%20teachers.pdf.

Suicide Prevention Resource Center. (2014). Suicidal behavior and acculturation among Hispanics in the United States. Retrieved from, http://www.sprc.org/news/suicidal-behavior-and-acculturation-among-hispanics-united-states.

Schmidtke, A., & Häfner, H. (1988). The Werther Effect after television films: New evidence for an old hypothesis. Psychol Med 18 (3): 665-76. doi: 10.1017/s0033291700008345.

Sheridan, Michael. (2011). Minnesota teen Haylee Fentress and Paige Moravetz kill selves during sleepover in 'suicide-pact.' Retrieved from, http://www.nydailynews.com/news/national/minnesota-teens-haylee-fentress-paige-moravetz-kill-sleepover-suicide-pact-article-1.113822.

Thestar.com. (2017). First nations suicide epidemic in Northern Ohio requires immediate action: Nault. Retrieved from https://www.thestar.com/opinion/commentary/2017/07/24/first-nations-suicide-epidemic-in-northern-ontario-requires-immediate-action-nault.html.

USA Today. (2017). Suicide-related searchers surged after the release of "13 Reasons Why." Life. Retrieved from https://www.usatoday.com/story/life/tv/2017/07/31/13-reasons--might-have-triggered-suicide-searches-online/104160074/.

World Health Organization. (2017). Mental Health. Suicide Data. Retrieved from http://www.who.int/mental_health/prevention/suicide/suicideprevent/en/.

Zuckerman, D., Miller, S., Levin, M., & Jury, J, N. (2017). Do antidepressants increase suicide attempts? Do they have other risks? National Center For Health Research. Retrieved from, http://www.center4research.org/antidepressants-increase-suicide-attempts-risks/.

About the author

Támara Hill, MS, NCC, CCTP LPC, is a licensed therapist, nationally certified counselor, and certified trauma professional in a group private practice in Pennsylvania. She is certified by the International Association of Trauma Professionals and recognizes Dr. Eric Gentry's clinical theories as the foundation of her trauma-focused work. She specializes in working with children and adolescents suffering from mood disorders, emotional trauma, and disruptive behavioral disorders. She also occasionally sees parents, families, and young adults struggling with life transitions, grief, and loss. Tamara credits her career passion to a "divine calling" and is internationally recognized for corresponding literary works as well as appearances on radio, podcasts, webinars, and other media platforms.

Tamara is a family consultant, advocate within the community, and practice owner of Anchored Child & Family Counseling at www.anchoredinknowledge.com.

Made in the USA
San Bernardino, CA
14 June 2018